The Life That Brightens the Light

by
Rodric D. King

CCB Publishing
British Columbia, Canada

The Life That Brightens the Light

Copyright ©2022 by Rodric D. King
ISBN-13   978-1-77143-551-2
First Edition

Library and Archives Canada Cataloguing in Publication
King, Rodric D., author
The life that brightens the light / by Rodric D. King. -- First edition.
Issued in print and electronic formats.
ISBN 978-1-77143-551-2 (pbk.).--ISBN 978-1-77143-552-9 (pdf)
Additional cataloguing data available from Library and Archives Canada

Front cover photo credit: Jervaris Kirkland
Back cover photo credits: Jervaris Kirkland and Rodric D. King
Book cover creator: Rodric D. King

Extreme care has been taken by the author to ensure that all information presented in this book is accurate and up to date at the time of publishing. Neither the author nor the publisher can be held responsible for any errors or omissions. Additionally, neither is any liability assumed for damages resulting from the use of the information contained herein.

All rights reserved. No part of this publication may be reproduced, stored in a retrieval system or transmitted in any form or by any means, electronic, mechanical, photocopying, recording or otherwise without the express written permission of the author. If you would like to use material from the book, other than for review purposes, prior written permission must be obtained by contacting the author or publisher. Thank you for your support of the author's rights.

Author contact information:
Facebook: https://www.facebook.com/rodric.d.king
Phone: 407-819-6957

Publisher: CCB Publishing
             British Columbia, Canada
             www.ccbpublishing.com

DEDICATION

This book is dedicated to my two daughters, Danasha and Rodricka. When my children were born, and most definitely when their mom and I separated, I had an idea. My idea was to use my life, time, energy, and resources to build businesses that could be passed down to my children before I moved on. I am building an empire just for them. I don't want them to be an employee--I want them to be the employer. I knew if I became a wealthy man, I could cover all of my children's expenses while simultaneously teaching them everything they need to know to become wealthy on their own. That was and still is the plan.

I have a saying that I've been citing for years that goes like this: "I never would have had children if I had known there would have been a day that I would wake up and they were not in the same household as me." I fell victim to a major deception. I didn't understand that every father does NOT just decide to walk out on his children. I didn't stop to think to myself, "What if the relationship doesn't work?"

When people are young and inexperienced, they often rush into a relationship without understanding what it takes to make it work. In retrospect, I was too young at the time that I met the mother of my future children and believed love could conquer all. Sadly I was too inexperienced to know what I was doing or deciding. This could have been avoided with some parental guidance that I didn't have because I was raised in foster care. We were two totally different people with two totally different paths in life.

I've come to realize that in some cases, there are numbers of black fathers who are separated from their children due to breakups. With that said, I did the best I could to be a good and supportive father from a distance. It didn't matter how far I was over the road--I'd always come back to see my children and spend time. I didn't want to be the type of parent that just kept my children alive. I wanted the best for them even if it meant I had to personally do the impossible and sometimes go outside of my own comfort zone. I was and have always been willing to learn, grow, and develop into the person I need to be in order to feed them the best information and knowledge, as well as to give them an upper hand when they become adults. However, being broke and homeless didn't make my ability to parent easy, but I did what I could while working on building a life.

Again, I didn't have parental guidance as a teenager or young adult, and I was going to be sure my children didn't experience this as well. I wanted to be sure my children were being prepared for adulthood. It is very difficult to accept that my children were being raised without having maximum exposure to a winning mindset and seeing a good example of what success is and what it takes. This hurt me a lot because I feel like I failed my children as a father. I also don't like the idea of another man not only being around my children, but also raising them (if present counts as raising). However, the circumstances didn't permit me to be the father I knew I could be. So, I am dedicating this book to them because a ton of the principals I wanted them to learn are contained in this book.

When and if my children ever read this book I want them to know that they are truly loved and they have power in their decisions. They can always start over; they might not have the ability to start the clock over, but they can decide to be a better person than they were yesterday. I want them to follow the desires of their hearts based on the knowledge they gain about every decision and every opportunity they have and create. I want them to be themselves despite what the world thinks and to use their "limited" time wisely. That's why this book is dedicated to them. I want them to read this book as adults and take control over their lives and decisions and impact this world in their own way. That would make me just as proud as if I had been there for them the way I would've liked. Be great. Be strong. Be amazing ladies.

Love,
Daddy

Contents

Foreword vii

Introduction – "Can I Change?" ix

Chapter 1   My Personal Life – "Becoming A Singer" 1

Chapter 2   My Personal Life – "Release Day" 17

Chapter 3   My Personal Life – "Madison" 25

Chapter 4   Extreme Power Concept – "What Is the Extreme Power Concept?" 57

Chapter 5   Knowledge of Self – "What Is the Power in Self-Awareness?" 85

Chapter 6   Strategy – "Priorities" 99

Chapter 7   Strategy – "Goals and Plan" 109

Chapter 8   Strategy – "Daily Agenda" 121

Chapter 9   Mindset Control - "Conscious & Subconscious Mind" 128

Chapter 10 Mindset Control – "Hypnosis" 140

Chapter 11 Closing Statement – "The End" 149

Foreword

I am so grateful to have the pleasure of writing this foreword for my brother, my friend, and confidant Rodric King.

I have had the pleasure of knowing Rodric since we were pre-school aged kids. He once lived in the same neighborhood as my grandmother. Every weekend, holiday, or vacation that I would visit my grandmother, Rodric would come trotting down the street so that he, I, and the other neighborhood kids could hang out. My grandmother's house was the little blue house in the middle of the entire neighborhood; needless to say, that became the hangout spot.

Rodric has always been the kind of kid with the big personality and full of emotions. He was the explorer type who was always on a mission to figure out how to accomplish something in the neighborhood. Every day that the sun would come up, you could see Rodric playing in his yard then after breakfast; like clockwork, you would see Rodric wearing cut off jean-shorts with a stick or something in his hands, skipping or walking extremely fast to my grandma's house to see if I could come out to play or if he could come inside. That went on for years to the point to where-in we looked for him to come to the house every day.

After a while, Rodric would leave my grandmother's house and go find something to get into. He was a very inquisitive kid that always yearned for knowledge. He would always get into something; to the point to where, you would always see him running home at some point because he did something to bother someone for their attention. Today that has not changed.

Rodric is a great father and entrepreneur who works very hard to gain the attention of his peers and his fans. He loves to spread knowledge and help others more than he helps himself. He has always been the type to study something until he masters it. Rodric has always been amazing in his own right. I have always told him that he will be a multi-millionaire one day and that he will be internationally known;

well, I was right. He has amazed me and many of his peers with his many accomplishments. Not only has he grown in his career, but he has also grown as a man, and it shows.

I am more than elated to have the opportunity to watch the person who I knew as a child grow into someone that the world loves and adores. Not only is the world getting a great guy, but they are also getting a jack of all trades, master of many. Now let me have the pleasure of introducing one of my favorite people in the world the teacher, the singer, the father, the pilot, and the author Rodric King…

Latoya Oates, MA, RMHCI, PLC

Introduction

"Can I Change?"

You have decided to invest your time into reading this book because something within you is looking to change. The content contained in this book will force you to think outside the box. You will be forced to change in ways that may be challenging or uncomfortable. A conscious decision to change is the beginning, but it isn't enough because we, as humans, forget. The wind can blow, and you'll go into a new direction unless a decision to make a change in your life is deeply rooted.

In order for this book to have its greatest impact on you, you must have a strong desire to change. Why do you want to change? What you're currently doing with your life may not be giving you the results you want. Maybe you feel you could obtain or create more for yourself. Either way, you are right! *more? meh, better, less is okay 4/17*

I wanted a lot out of life before my mind changed. I couldn't contrive the true desires of my heart until my mind changed which you'll see as I begin to share my life experiences. I was getting exactly what I was asking for which was the "undesired." I complained about everything. I learned the hard way to always be attentive to what you give your attention to because you can expect to receive more of it. This is exactly why complaining is a horrible activity. *Yes!*

Here is a phrase you will see a lot in this book. "What you focus on expands." After reading this book, this phrase will be a part of your new mental makeup. This simply means you can expect to receive more of what you are thinking about, talking about, and giving your energy too.

This book deals with my personal experiences, the extreme power concept, which I created, the laws of attraction, the conscious and subconscious mind, and hypnosis. I want you to know that majority of the information shared in this book is foundational information (very basic). Be sure to conduct more research on these topics because my job is to lead you to the water, but it's up to you to drink.

This book is for those who are uncomfortable and know there is more to life, but have no idea how to obtain it. It is also for those with dreams and visions. These are individuals who know they must continue to grow and develop, but need guidance. I am going to help the clouds in that vision to blow away. There is an approach to help you know and understand where you are going and why. This book is going to give you step-by-step instructions. Of all the nuggets in this book, I am sure something is going to impact you in a way that causes a major shift in your life. Let's start with my journey to becoming a professional singer because you'll see how I applied specific principles in order to obtain the true desires of my heart. You'll be able to apply these same principles to your own life.

Chapter 1

My Personal Life

"Becoming A Singer"

*T*his is my story about my journey to becoming a professional singer. I knew as I was going through this process that I would write about my experience. I had you in mind for a very long time. You will learn that your mess can be your message. So, I want my story to inspire and enlighten those who wish to reach their greatest potential.

I was born on May 17, 1984, and raised in Jacksonville, Florida. I was adopted as an infant, but my adopted mother went to heaven in 1996. I was only 12 years old when she left us on Mother's Day, and she was buried on my birthday. Yes, it was as sad as it sounds.

This is the only picture in the world
that exists with me as a child.

The Life That Brightens the Light

Afterwards, I was immediately placed into the foster care system, but not before having to protect myself from my adopted mother's grieving brother. He was somewhat abusive and I was removed from the home after beating him with a stick. He always found a reason to whoop me, and I got tired of it.

Once I was placed into the foster care system, I went from house-to-house for a bit. I survived and graduated high school in May of 2003 only because I loved basketball. I had to maintain good grades in order to play. However, I didn't get the privilege to walk or attend the prom because I transferred every uncomfortable emotion into anger and battered two students badly. As a result of this incident, I was jailed for six months and charged with simple battery because it was on school property.

That arrest at 18 years old completely destroyed my opportunity to go to the military as I had planned since 1999. I invested so much time in our JROTC program at my school with a purpose, but I was unsuccessful because the arrest disqualified me. Once I aged out of the foster care system, I was paid to go to college as a ward of the state of Florida. When college was completed, I was homeless off and on for the majority of my adult life--at least up to the point of this book. I have launched many businesses, and 97% of the businesses I started failed between 2003 and 2016. I have lost a great deal of money on network marketing programs and real estate seminars and programs. I learned not to be afraid of risk, but it came at an expensive cost. Literally!

I became an adult without a lot of the basic knowledge I needed to survive in this country. I had a suspended driver's license, child support, back taxes due, bad/no credit, a criminal record, no stable income, vague knowledge of being a responsible adult, and two toddlers Let's put it this way: it was rough getting back to zero. I've worked for major corporations and made it to the top only to be disgusted with the time I was losing. I needed a change and a job wasn't it. I learned what my true asset was. I found out that singing would be fun if it were a profession. That became my priority.

I started with the idea of becoming a rapper. There were way too many people rapping, so I was turned on to the idea of becoming a singer. I had a friend who was a singer. He wasn't a professional, but he made it look cool. So, now that you have a piece of whom I am, let's get into the message of this book.

My saying is, "You will NEVER discover your true potential until you discover your true potential." I truly believe when people learn the thought process behind my intentions; they can use some of these methods to live a life with more peace, success, and confidence.

To be completely open and honest with you, this book would be a great success if people lives were influenced by the choices I've made in my own life. Again, in the back of my mind, I knew I'd tell my story and this helped me to endure the trials and tribulations associated with my decisions. I will explain all the concepts I adopted and applied to my own circumstances. My hope is that they impact you in a positive manner.

I'm calling this section, "The Spark" because most people are never really prepared to change or take a different course in life until they hit the breaking point, rock bottom, or something impactful happens to them. These three possible events are what I call, "The Spark." The spark for me was my divorce back in 2015. My wife left me, and it disturbed me emotionally, but I didn't allow these emotions to linger too long. I'd followed motivational content for years prior to my divorce, so I had everything I needed in me. At first I was torn apart because I knew I would have to accept the fact that things would be different without my partner. I did a lot of things wrong in that marriage and I didn't expect my marriage to be temporary, but I had to move on. I had a choice. Remember, when you approach a circumstance, you have three choices. You can approach your crossroad with positivity, negativity, or try to ignore the circumstance all together.

I realized my options, and one was to stay hurt and become unproductive. That wasn't a good option because if she secretly checked on me years later and I hadn't accomplished anything, she could say, "I dodged a bullet." Nope, I wasn't having that. The second option I had was to become something outstanding using all the emotions that were created with the divorce. I could do something great, but how? I decided to use the emotions that were already stirred up inside of me to propel myself forward. I was going to get my life together.

Let's think about that!

When you are traveling and you are going over the road, you MUST fill the car up with fuel, right? You know you are going to run out of fuel more than once, right? So, ideally, you want to reduce the amount of times you have to refuel by filling up your tank. You CANNOT run the vehicle long distance or locally without energy and power. That's why we use cars and trucks because of the benefits of having a power plant--the engine.

You have to buy the fuel, and it runs out. However, the benefits are that they propel us on and over the roadways to move and travel near and far. What's the point?

When you are tired or sleepy, you cannot produce. You won't move or perform productively. Therefore, you need energy, food, and rest. In this case, the divorce gave me emotions. Those emotions could have drained my energy, or I could use the emotions as motivation. This motivation was a source of energy--fuel. It gave me the ability to spend an excessive amount of time, concentration, and focus on whatever I chose to entertain. This is similar to the example of filling up a car before going on a long journey.

You need energy, motivation, power, and everything in between to attack what is believed to be impossible. Think about the tools you'll learn in the later chapters. You'll understand the extreme power concept, the conscious and subconscious mind, and hypnosis. This will help define who you are, identifying your strengths, using the law of attraction and the law of polarity. You need all these tools on your journey to success just as you'd change the oil, check the tires, pack the car with valuables, and fill up on fuel before hitting the road.

If you know how supplying power works, you can understand the more energy that's required for the task the bigger the power plant must be in order to have sufficient power. You can't have huge plans without the energy required to hit and obtain your goals. You need every bit of additional power you can pull. Every piece of information in this book will ensure you are equipped.

Let's get back to the topic.

I used the emotions from my divorce and transferred those emotions to positive energy and used that energy in the form of motivation to propel myself in a specific direction. In this case, the direction was determined by my priorities, goals, plans, and agenda, which you'll also learn in a later chapter.

As a foster child, children that weren't blood-related always surrounded me and this created a standoff-ish attitude. I didn't want my belongings stolen, so I had to always appear tough. Therefore, when I was hurt or embarrassed, I NEVER showed those emotions. I reprogrammed those emotions and turned them into anger. I had to learn how to express those feelings as an adult because I couldn't express them as a child.

Side Note:

If you are dealing with unruly children, this is something to think about. Every problem child isn't necessarily a problem child. You need to help these children identity their emotions and show them it is okay to express how they are feeling. They just need to learn how to do so.

Here is the point. I learned at a very young age that you could rewire your feelings and emotions. We had that kind of control. That is exactly what I did with my emotions from my divorce.

I said to myself, "Everything that my ex-wife ever called me that was considered bad or undesirable is what I will change." I said to myself, "I will change everything she pointed out in order to make me a better person, and when I am successful, I will identify the specific thoughts and principles that created more success for my life (i.e. this book). Thus, I will prove her wrong about leaving me." This is something you must realize. Tell yourself what you must to choose the correct path. Get your mind in the game.

We can agree that my motivation was a little off center, but I was completely honest with myself for a good reason. What if she was right about my character? What if she was saying these things out of anger? Who would I really be hurting if I didn't change? I most definitely wouldn't be hurting her if I did or did not change. It sounds like I used reverse psychology on myself, right? I chose a positive direction, and I am currently reaping the benefits of all my decisions. She has impacted my life in a very positive way. She gets that credit.

I quickly began the development process; I needed to grow in spirit, my character, and my mentality. My idea was to completely reinvent myself and simply upgrade myself to the new me along with my life and my circumstances. I needed to search myself, and I did. Do NOT ignore the fact that I upgraded myself. Look in the mirror.

Always remember, when you want to change your reality, you cannot do so by cutting the apples off the tree and then expecting a different harvest. You need to plant different seeds. The searching portion of this phase was me. I had to dig into the soil trying to find out what seeds I had planted in order to realize what the harvest used to be. Then I could put new seeds into the soil. This was my process, and this is why you have to look at yourself first when you want to bring change to your life. Start with the soil--your mind.

I questioned everything in my life and existence. I wanted to be free from my debt and didn't want to worry about financial stability. I wanted my driver's license back and to be free from child support stress. I wanted to quit smoking cigarettes, workout, and eat healthier. I wanted to go back to school and grow my hair out, but it would NEVER grow. I didn't want to worry about any of the things my ex-wife and I had to deal with as a couple. I wanted to be free from the criminal charges I was facing at the time which were driver's license related charges. They were seriously holding me back, and she felt the hardship of all these personal issues. I wanted to find and pursue my passion, but I had a lot going on. I was so self-sabotaging. I almost don't blame her for leaving.

How often do we realize we want so much, but get only the opposite? Are you tired of it? The conscious mind can conjure what it pleases, but if the seeds aren't correct or corrected, you'll continue to get the same things.

In March 2015, I worked it out with my soon to be ex-wife to take one of the two cars we owned. I knew the car would make it easier for me to disappear out of her life because I could sleep in the vehicle. Immediately after our agreement, I moved all of my property into the vehicle and took off. I was kind of happy because I knew I would do something totally different with my life. At the time, I was working for AAA National Headquarters. If you know me, I hate trading time for money. This needed to change immediately. This wasn't something I chose to do, but my ex-wife wanted stability and music wasn't doing it. I went back into the workforce to honor her wishes. I wanted to quit so badly, but I was too big of a coward to just do it. I had the car and that steady paycheck. That paycheck was difficult to give up especially when child support was on my back. Look at my situation. Homeless, living in a car, and currently driving while my license was suspended with pending charges and on probation. Ugly, right? Also, I noticed a trend. I was only able to pay child support when I had a partner. My partners usually absorbed some, if not all, the cost associated with living stability giving me the freedom to maintain a job because I had a place to sleep.

The paycheck from AAA National Headquarters was keeping me out of jail because I had to pay probation on a weekly basis or go back to jail as I picked up a new charge of Violation of Probation. Child support wasn't giving me a break at all, and probation had its weekly and monthly dues, which were taken out of my check before I got it. I had this thing in the back of my head that kept saying, "Your wife also didn't like the fact that you weren't a strong financial provider for your household because of child support, so that is why she wanted out." They began taking child support out of her income. If that was or wasn't the case, I understood her position. I began sharing my plans with my close friend at work. I told him I wanted to travel the country while singing everywhere until I was a paid full-time singer. That was one of the priorities. He had a lot of questions such as, "Where would

The Life That Brightens the Light

you stay," "How would you generate an income," and "What if you got sick?" I had an answer for everything. He was more impressed than shocked, and I respected his opinion a lot.

This was my desk at AAA National Headquarters.

I was looking for the right time to give up the income I was earning at AAA National Headquarters. I finally figured out how to do it. I decided I'd take the little money I was making and record a single and sell it while I was out on the road. I would hustle my product like my life depended on it because it did. I did some figures on a piece of paper to see what the potential was of this becoming a reality. I was discouraged at first because I was parking my car on the property of AAA National Headquarters at night to get some sleep for work the next day. I showered at L.A. Fitness every day and washed my clothes at a friends' house. Why would I spend this little bit of money I have on recording a new song under these circumstances? I didn't even know anyone with a studio to record. If I decided to do the song, I wouldn't do it unless they had the best quality, but good quality comes at a cost. I had to make a decision to pull the trigger and burn my boat because there was no going back. I was willing to give up the paycheck because the child support deductions weren't leaving me enough income to maintain stability anyway. I preferred to die versus living like a slave the rest of my life.

I decided to entertain the idea because I drew up some pretty good scenarios. I used the "Priorities, Goals, Plan, & Agenda system" to contrive a solid strategy. You will learn everything there is to know about this system in the later chapters. I was also implementing the principal of "What you focus on expands." I could make the money back that was spent on the recording if I hustled my butt off. If I hustled hard enough, I could even realize some profits. I was already living out of my car while on probation for "driving while license is suspended," so I was motivated. I conducted the research necessary to find a studio I could afford. I was broke, but I saved the money necessary to payoff everything I needed to complete the new recording. I made the decision NOT to pay child support in order to aggressively save. There were many nights I didn't eat or I was forced to panhandle in order to eat and cover fuel cost, but all I cared about was being sure the studio owner was paid in full, upfront. The owner and I built the track and recorded the song titled "Pushing." It took me less than two weeks to do what was required of me. Keep in mind, I was going to work every day and showering at L.A. Fitness daily. Instead of keeping money for food and fuel, I was spending every dime for this new single.

I reached a point in my progress where I was done with my role in the development of the song. Now I was waiting for the studio owner to produce the music with what is known as "the mix and master" of the track. This guy knew I lived out of my car. He knew my license was suspended. He knew child support didn't leave me enough money to support myself. He knew I showered at L.A. Fitness. He knew I slept outside of my job. He knew I was spending every single dime to complete this project with him in order to turn around and sell it for a profit in order to get my initial investment back. He knew I didn't save a penny for myself for food or fuel.

Can you believe he gave me the run around for nearly two months? Yes, two months of my circumstance due to someone else's efforts or the lack thereof. He never produced the music I had paid him for, and

The Life That Brightens the Light

he became defensive that I was rushing him even though I was kind and very patient. According to him, he took even more time producing the track because I rushed him. I desperately needed the track in order to begin making the money back that I spent with him. I called him before work on May 24, 2015, and he cursed me out for calling him back-to-back. I was totally offended. I literally wanted him dead.

Side Note:

I was being very transparent. I couldn't believe after all the sacrifices I made and all the obstacles I overcame that he would be the one to hold from me the very thing I was going to use to turn my life around. I was in a bad place mentally. Everything I was going through was concentrated on him. Everything in my life was evolving around his work; he knew this.

When he cursed me out on the phone, the timing was in his favor because I was going to work at the time. I decided I'd handle him right after work. I had planned to get off from work and follow him home. My best friend from work offered me left overs he had at the house. He told me to come by after work to pick it up. I knew I didn't have the funds to feed myself, so I would handle the studio owner immediately after I picked up the food. The problem was I didn't get off until 11:30 p.m., which meant I couldn't get to his house until midnight. He was fine with that though.

I got off that night and pulled out my big "Pakistanian 440a Super Stainless-Steel Ranger." I placed that in the seat next to me because I had nothing to lose and this studio owner took the wrong person for granted. In my mind, he had to pay. I left AAA National Headquarters property and headed for my co-worker's residence. I was calling my co-worker while I was on route to his residence because I was texting him during the last hour I was on the clock. He didn't respond to one message. I was hungry, and I remembered him reassuring me that midnight wasn't too late for me to go there. I eventually got to his house and he didn't answer the door or the phone. I was so angry. I felt like it only made my rage worst. I ran the doorbell, called, and even banged on the door a little bit. I never made contact with him.

I began to head in the direction of the studio, but I decided to use the last of my change to buy a black n' mild. Yeah, I was still a smoker at this time in my life. I stopped at the closest gas station adjacent to my friend's house. After I made my purchase, I hopped in the car and left the gas station. It was about 1:00 a.m. and within a mile of the gas station when I began to approach two police cars waiting to exit the entrance of a shopping center that was empty and blacked out. There was more than enough time and space for them to pull out and leave, but I got the impression they were waiting on my vehicle to pass. I barely passed their vehicles when they shot out behind me, and within seconds, their emergency lighting packages were illuminated. I have enough knowledge to know to pull into a legal parking spot so that when I go to jail, they wouldn't have the car towed. I went to jail because my license was currently suspended, and I was on probation for the same charge in another county. However, the car wasn't towed.

While in jail, I wrote my friend/co-worker all the information he needed to find the keys to the car along with information about where the car could be stored. I spent two months in one county, and after completing the time for that county, I was transferred to the other county and spent an additional two months in jail there. I did a total of four months in jail in two different counties. You probably think that was a bad circumstance or you're thinking I deserved it. Well, this was all a part of my journey. It happened because it was supposed to happen. Think about it.

I couldn't leave Florida for California while on probation. That would have ended just as badly if not worse. When you are on probation you are not allowed to leave the county, state, or whatever the terms are in that jurisdiction. In addition, remember I couldn't easily give up the income that AAA National Headquarters was paying. Well, it was gone now! All of my property in the car sustained rain damage because my friend didn't know how to close my sunroof. In addition, I was free of all the charges meaning no charges were lingering or pending. I was free and clear. To add to the greatness of this horrible experience, I couldn't smoke in jail. So, when I got out, I just didn't pick it up. I hadn't smoked in four months. In addition, I worked out a lot in jail and ate healthier. It was a balanced diet. Think about that!

Those were nearly all the things I voiced as something I wanted to address. Forcefully, the issues were cured and when I was released, I left with a solid plan that marinated for four months. The entire four months I was in jail, I was plotting a strategic plan for the day I was released (I used the "Priorities, Goals, Plans and Daily Agenda" system). I had to draft a plan so airtight it would have been impossible NOT to obtain my priorities. It took every day of those four months to construct this plan in grave detail, and I had nothing but time while incarcerated. I even had a detailed list along with the order of topics I would research once I was free. I wanted to work a job that wasn't difficult to walk into every day in the name of freedom. It is a double whammy to go to a job you don't like and have the income you make taken away forcefully. I wanted a role or position that didn't feel like work that could pay enough so I could be financially stable. I decided to focus and concentrate my efforts on becoming a paid full-time singer. I had no idea how it would come true, but I knew what I would do to create the opportunities because I had a rock solid plan. I needed to be heavily exposed nationally. I was applying the principle "What you focus on expands."

You see when the subconscious decision was accepted, the universe, GOD, and fate did EVERYTHING required to position me to win. Everything I desired I received by way of these circumstances. I couldn't look at my previous circumstances as a bad thing or experience. Steve Jobs said, "You can't connect the dots looking forward. You can only connect the dots looking back." Well, thank goodness, I am a super-positive person because I had no idea why my life was turned upside down after the divorce. I only knew my life was going to change and I didn't care how bad things seemed. I was determined to have the difference I expected. I got what I needed. Change!

The decision and the desire to change were buried deep down inside my heart. The subconscious mind could accept this new policy in which it would operate and work closely with the universe to open the doors required to get the results I desired, even if it seemed unfavorable. Be careful what you ask for.

You must have that attitude. You need that approach. It works. You want everything working in your favor. When you put all these forces in and under your subconscious command, you get what you want. You must ask yourself, "What do I really want out of life?" Be specific. If you don't know what you want, you have a big problem. Do you remember the example of going over the road? You must get the oil changed, pack the car with the things you'll need, check the tires, get a tune up, and fill the car with fuel just before you take off. All these things must be done for this journey to have the opportunity to be a success.

Do you see all the tools used in my journey just to get my journey from negative twenty to zero? I searched for a better version of me and found him. I used and deployed helpful principles. I changed the seeds in the soil. I created a plan. I stayed focused on the development of that plan for four months. I listed exactly what I wanted. I converted emotions into positive energy in order to push myself. I remained positive throughout an experience most would have viewed as unfortunate circumstances. After surviving the circumstances, I identified how the dots connected looking back. The law of attraction did the rest by giving me the desires I listed. These disadvantages were in my way of having a solid foundation to become a professional singer, which was the priority. Now, back to the story.

How was I going to become a professional singer? I knew I needed exposure build a following and fan base. At the time I was known, but in only two or three major cities. I knew if I increased my exposure, my chances of making money as a fulltime singer would be more realistic. So I talked to the educated people near me in jail. I had to start where I was, right? I just needed ideas. Any information was more than what I had. After talking to different people, I found a method of making some legal money but at a great risk to my health. I was going to do clinical trials. That's right! I was at the point where I was willing to risk my health to get ahead. Don't get me wrong--it wasn't the best idea, but it paid very well.

The lifestyle was traveling to different cities and states to attempt a clinical trial where they test drugs on you that haven't been passed yet. They give you all the details about the drug, what to expect, where you would stay, how long you would stay, and other information about the trial upfront so you can make a decision whether this was something you want to do or not. It required a lot of research to find companies that offered trials, dates that matched your schedule, and locations that worked. I was basically going to book myself around the U.S. in these trials one after another.

A great example of the compensation was $10,000 for two months on one trial, $2,500 for three weeks doing another trial, and maybe $1,500 in two days for doing this trial. I didn't believe this person at first, but I knew this was my ticket if he wasn't lying. Money was the answer to my immediate problems. I needed to make enough to invest into some real plans and to get child support caught up or paid off because I knew while I was in jail, I fell behind again.

I contrived plans in order to cover all the bases and to incorporate the clinical trials along with the priority--singing. It took four months to figure everything out in complete detail, but I had a plan. That is always a start. My plan ended with me eventually becoming a full-time singer, being financially stable, getting my drivers back, getting a passport, child support paid in full, publishing this book and having well over 19,000+ subscribers on YouTube. I had much bigger dreams, but those dreams felt impossible being homeless all the time while living on the street. It was so hard for me as an adult; I needed a plan in order to become stable.

Stable is zero. I can be financially stable with a job, but the job gets old. It takes a ton of your time, and you get tired of going to the same place day after day and getting paid peanuts. A job robbed me of ALL MY TIME. I couldn't build my dream losing, wasting, or trading time for money. I was building someone else's dream working a job. I found something I loved to do. Singing was the ticket for me, and I wouldn't be denied. The spark was moving me in the right direction, and I've seen the results since the initial spark. I am so grateful for the spark.

Let's side track a bit.

You will notice my plan didn't always go as it was originally planned. Remember, it is okay when your plans are derailed because as I continued to work my plan they eventually made more sense after the circumstances changed everything. The plan evolves and becomes more practical as you continue to develop and work it. You just might experience this, but the most important thing is to start with a detailed strategic plan. Then, you should continue working your plan, updating, and evaluating it. The plan will come together. It'll eventually make sense and become more practical.

Have you ever built a detailed, strategic plan for your personal or business life? Have you experienced circumstances that altered your plans? Did you give up or keep pushing through the dead ends? Did you continue to evaluate your plans? In the later chapters, I am going to dive head first into the Priority, Goals, Plans, and Daily Agenda system.

So, have you had your spark yet? When was your spark? Have there been positive results since your spark or did your trajectory never change? When you are at rock bottom there is nowhere to go, but up. Again, just get a plan and start working it. Stick with the plan. It took years to get the results I desired.

Here is a good example of that:

I remember when I used to job hunt. Job-hunting isn't a simple task and a job itself that you must treat it as such. You must have a plan. You must know what you are looking for or at least have an idea. You must be realistic. I used to put in a lot of hours applying at jobs. I'd put in for jobs I wasn't interested in, but if I were hired I was fine with the duties for the pay. A good example of this was my resume that was constructed for administrative work. If I saw a construction position with a decent pay, I'd apply.

The point is this, put a TON of effort into your plan on a consistent basis. Construction of a detailed, strategic plan is a job! Work it! In the next chapter, I am going to tell you what happened on release day.

Chapter 2

My Personal Life

"Release Day"

Finally, the day of my release came, and I was ready for a brand new path. I had all my plans tabulated, and there was a ton of research I needed to conduct. The clinical trials were at the top of my list because this is what would pay for my stability and business ventures. Before I did any of that, I needed to check my pay card to verify my last paycheck was paid out. I had a little over two hundred dollars to my name. That was more than enough to pay for a trip out of Orlando, Florida. I finally called my friend/co-worker, and he was excited to know that I had been released.

I immediately went to his house to check on my property and caught up with him a little. This was a great man. He, like many other friends I grew to know, had brought me into their households while their own family existed within the home. I am thankful that these special men in my life who trusted me. (Lewis Heyward, Evan Alcala, Lee H, and Nestor Cardona.) I would never betray their openness or mistreat or mistake their kindness for weakness or violate that trust. I seriously appreciate you guys.

I met up with Lee, and I explained to him what all of my plans were because I understood sometimes you can move someone in, but you can never get them out. I wasn't there to be an inconvenience. I would sleep on the street before making his life harder. He made it clear how much he respected me for the journey I was willing to take to achieve success. Both he and his wife decided I could stay at their house for two weeks since that's how long it would be before my bus departed for Madison. I am sure Madison, Wisconsin, may seem like a very specific location. No, it's not Atlanta, New York, Miami, Los Angeles or Las Vegas.

I found and scheduled my appointment for a clinical trial and was leaving Orlando, Florida for Madison on September 29, 2015. I was super excited because I'd never been to Madison, the capitol of Wisconsin. I had plans and still had no idea what to expect because I was going to be in a different city and state that was foreign to me, and I wouldn't know one person. Being September, the temperatures would be much different than Florida. I failed to realize at the time how far north the state of Wisconsin actually was, and I arrived on October 1, 2015. Temperatures easily dropped below freezing, and I didn't have a place to sleep. Do you think I was worried about that? Not one bit. I had this understanding that you don't always need all the answers. This prevents you from giving up or stressing about the things that are out of your control.

Gear given to me by my college friends.

Side Note:

This is a very important lesson to learn. You DO NOT need all the answers, at least not all of the time. Also, NEVER worry about the things you cannot control. It takes away your focus, concentration and energy from the things you can control. What good will it do if you are giving your time and energy to something thing that is out of your control? Instead, use it for something you can control and use it for a greater purpose.

I knew I wouldn't always feel like singing to generate an income, and I knew singing wouldn't always work in every city and state to generate an income on the streets, which you'll notice. During the two weeks I conducted a lot of research trying to learn as much about Madison as I possibly could. This wasn't my first rodeo of just spontaneously leaving a city for a random state. Back in 2009, I left my hometown for good and have never looked back. I went from Jacksonville, Florida to Atlanta, Georgia. I left Jacksonville the moment I realized I wanted to learn how to sing. I knew I could be anything I put my mind to, and I was set on becoming a recording artist or a professional vocalist. That will be a movie, documentary, or another book.

The first thing I did when I traveled from state-to-state as a homeless man was place an ad on Craigslist (when the platform was relevant) along with multiple other websites advertising my ability to "Vocally Train" anyone and "Train Kids" in fundamental basketball skills. Sometimes, I'd focus more on one than the others and in Madison; it was the "General Laborer For Hire" ad, which was more popular in Madison. Here is the exact ad I wrote (word for word):

Laborer For Hire (Ready Right Now)

What can I do? Everything! Put me to work.

Hello,

My name is Rodric, and I am new to Madison, Wisconsin. I'm currently an Independent Artist (Singer) that gets on the road and travel to different auditions and gigs nationally. I have a prolific plan for my vision to get where I'm going in life, but sometimes you need a little assistance. I am also a father of two daughters. I'm currently working a full-time job as a Personal Vocal Instructor, but I am looking to use my additional time to make extra income. (www.RodricKing.com)

The Life That Brightens the Light

You might wonder, "What kind of work would I have you do, Rodric?"

That's a great question because of the beauty of being a hard worker; I am willing to do it all. Anything!

Simply refer to the list below for all the assignments I'm ready and more than willing to complete for you. However, if you find that what you need isn't below, contact me with questions and all your concerns so I can address them directly. Thank you in advance for considering me.

Garage cleaning

Clean out room(s)

Rake yard(s)

Wash dishes

Pick up trash

Move furniture

Wash car/truck

Install/uninstall

Fuel vehicle(s)

Handy man

Labor

Clean gutters

Clean the house

Moving labor

Wash clothes

Cut grass

Store run

Clip hedges

Clean out closets

Yard edging

Assist with yard

Rodric King logo

Sales

Planting

Gardening

Carpet cleaning

Cook

Cut down trees

Take out trash

Organize

Painting

Take pictures

Dog walking

Read you the newspaper/book

Computer cleaning (virus/crash/slow/pop ups)

Sing for you (weddings, anniversaries)

Shampoo the car(s) interior

Assisting roof installation, planting/gardening

Clean the backyard

You name the job and I will come to work for YOU. All prices are negotiated between us. You name the price. I will agree or disagree. Simple! I am waiting by the phone. Just give me a call or click right now.

I will travel, but please consider the cost associated with traveling. We must be sure it's covered in our negotiations.

*(Disclaimer: The image or photograph featured in this advertisement has no association with the content in this ad or the request.)

I used a simple strategy. I asked myself, what do I need? How do I force what I need to come to me? I needed instant cash and opportunities that payout cash. I found a way for peoples' problems to become mine for a fee we both agreed too. I also found a way to make them come to me.

Side Note:

I discovered this concept due to my panhandling efforts. Occasionally, I'd panhandle, but I'd ask if they had some work I could do for a few dollars instead of begging. I figured ad's would make more sense. Always remember that simple plans can evolve into a stronger strategy if you keep working on it. Smart is taking something complicated and making it simple. Always be smart! This process started when I asked myself questions. Remember to question your approach and your process. Let's shift back to the story!

This advertisement generated a response in the Madison area an average man would only dream of. I was setting appointments before I left Florida. The income was waiting on me before I got there. I still had the car and a lot of property to store or get rid of. Luckily, for me, my ex-wife reached out to me asking for the car back because she lost the brand-new Camaro I bought her. I was more than happy to give it to her because after this last run-in with the law, I decided my plan wouldn't be effective if I was back in jail for "driving while license suspended" again. Let's just say I don't think the circumstances would be favorable this time around. I made a conscious decision to stay from behind the wheel for five years as required according to the courts. I was going to honor this so I could potentially get my license back in the future.

As it relates to homelessness, I have been homeless more than 65% of my adult life. In the past, I have been on the streets before with my children as well. I knew what I would and wouldn't need in order to survive out there in Madison. I tossed property that wouldn't help me and stored things that I wouldn't need. In addition, I realized my ex-wife didn't lose the Camaro because the guy she was sleeping with was showboating in the vehicle--at least that's what I was told. Not to mention this was the same guy we were renting a room out to when we were together. I found out a month after our separation that she was pregnant by him. I never brought it up to her. She wanted to turn the car in to clear her credit. The news didn't bother me one bit. I was on a mission.

Side Note:

Make a conscious effort to avoid individuals who are NOT on a mission. Did you notice this sensitive news could have angered me in many ways and I stated, "It didn't bother me one bit?" It didn't bother me because what was more important? Were her actions more important than my priorities? Of course not! Therefore, I knew where my attention needed to be concentrated. This is the point! Some people who are also known as, "low lives" have NOTHING to look forward to so they have time and energy to spend on anything entertaining to them. So, if I had nothing going on in my life imagine how I could have responded. If you spend time and energy with low lives you can expect to deal with a ton of petty circumstances. So, when I meet a person, I do not judge them, however I determine if they have goals and where they are in the pursuit of those priorities. This will save you a lot of time and energy. Trust me. For the record, low life sounds worst than it actually is. I am NOT looking down on these individuals or judging them. However, we must classify the type of people we wish to grant access too and this is a common term that is used in my culture. In addition, I am NOT insinuating goal oriented individuals will NOT be energy drainers or petty. Getting back on track.

Finally, I reduced my property down to clothes and hygienic products equaling only two heavy bags. I was proud of myself because I hate throwing away memories. At Lee's house, I stored documents, important tax information, clothes I would keep, along with other items.

At this point, the research was done, the tickets were booked, my property had been sorted, and it was time to depart. I got on the Greyhound and hit the road. I wrote a chapter or two of this book while

The Life That Brightens the Light

on that bus ride. At this time, while I was on the bus, I am more empowered than ever. I didn't care what the future held. I focused on the current emotions. I was free. I was happy. I was living. I was once again living outside of the box and outside of my comfort zone. That is the only place to truly grow and develop. I love it there.

A picture before the Megabus take-off.

You always want to find a way out of your comfort zone, but this is very easy when you have a rock solid plan. Trust me on this one. Think about it! You go through the entire Priorities, Goals, Plans, and Agenda System. This system will encourage you to list all the things you want to achieve in this lifetime. I am sure they are not simple, and I am guessing it will probably require additional education, skills, courses, licenses, permits and experience in some other areas in the arena of knowledge, right? This is uncharted territory for you, right? You are not comfortable until you gain the knowledge and get comfortable exercising the act, right? Always remember, if your priorities don't scare you, they aren't big enough.

The point is this--get outside of your elements and get outside of your comfort zone. Do the things that are uncomfortable and new. You will learn things you have not been exposed to yet. It is worth it. The next chapter will cover the trip to and the arrival into Madison, Wisconsin.

Chapter 3

My Personal Life

"Madison"

The drive from Orlando, Florida, to Madison, Wisconsin, was interesting. I conducted a lot of research on the bus and located a shelter where I could sleep for the night. I was scheduling dates for service to my clients on the ride there. I would arrive, but I'd give myself three days before servicing the first client to get into the shelter and get the area figured out. I found myself singing for food the first few days at The University of Wisconsin. Panhandling wasn't going to cut it because the city of Madison has a growing population of homeless people. The people of Madison didn't respond well to the homeless panhandling, at least not where I was operating. This is why it was necessary to have an alternative, which is always important. I planned for this upset. My primary out was the Clinical Trial, and the payoff was big--but only if I was accepted and successfully completed the trial. My secondary out was the clients that were waiting to be serviced. I planned my travel dates from Florida according to the appointment I created with the trial company in Madison. The next day it was time to make my appointment to the clinical trial company. I went through the process of applying. I did specific tests to see if I would be accepted. I was denied. It hurt like hell because I really needed the money they were offering. However, I didn't know that this trial paid out $157 if you were denied. That chump change came in handy. So, I had money for bus fare and food for now, but not for long. Do you see how things usually work out? I don't think I had more than $5 or $6 dollars before arriving at the clinical trial location. Don't think because you have little or nothing everything is over. You can still operate with little to nothing. You just have to know and believe that you can. There is no shortage of money in this world. Someone has it.

Connect with the right people when the circumstances require it. Did that sound like a "You should panhandle" pitch?

Side Note:

Most people asked me in the past, "Why don't you just go to your family for help?" These are my personal thoughts on this topic, and I am being very transparent. There are a few reasons. One is that strangers are usually more helpful and caring than a person who knows you. The second reason is due to the fact that I don't like asking my family when they have their own issues. This is NOT to say strangers don't have issues too. That is NOT what I am insinuating. However, I don't know most strangers' personal circumstances, so it is a little easier to ask for what I need. The third reason is that I wasn't raised with or around my biological family so I limit my dependency and reliance on them. I personally don't think an outsider is looked upon the same, and it doesn't matter how many times they tell me I am wrong about that idea. Also, I won't ask friends because I feel like my problems shouldn't be theirs, and I don't like bothering them about my needs. I need to stand on my own two feet. Most people run for help before there is even a real situation. I am not judging them. I am just showing the contrast. I am from the foster care system. We were forced to be independent. We usually felt like we were raising ourselves depending on the home and the experience. I am sure there are people who were in care that had a great upbringing. I was not one of them, but I am not complaining about my experience. It was what it was. Shall we move back to the story?

Finally, it's three days later, and I began servicing my clients. The timing couldn't have been any better because my singing hustle wasn't very successful. I was beginning to see how a hustle in one geographic location doesn't work as well as in other areas of the country. I'd find great places on the campus to sing, but security would run me off the property. I still built great relationships with students that attended the school, but that was about all. College kids definitely didn't have a lot of extra money to spend and most definitely not to give away. I tend to avoid panhandling in areas where the homeless exists. The constant exposure of homeless people influenced the mindsets of individuals in these areas. Where the homeless existed evoked a particular attitude, and it wasn't healthy for my purpose. So I knew better.

Besides, I had clients who needed service. I had a few individuals who needed their back yards clear of trash and debris. I connected with a client who needed his yard cut and another client who needed help painting. The client that stood out the most was a client that owned a few houses, and he was in the process of remodeling two of three houses he owned. One of the houses was a beautiful mansion. He had a lot of work for me. I scaled back on my marketing efforts and focused on the needs of this one new client. On the first day of work, the new client picked me up at an establishment where I spent a lot of time. The place was called "Porchlight Inc." This is one of the few locations in Madison where I utilized their facility along with all the resources that were available to me. Madison has a ton of valuable resources for their homeless community.

We went from Porchlight Inc. to my client's house where he was having the roof laid, but he didn't call professionals. He was doing it himself, and he required extra manpower. I was that extra manpower, and from time to time he'd hire extra bodies. We agreed on a price and a schedule. On the days he didn't feel like working, he would communicate that with me, and we made the necessary arrangements when he was ready to work. It was very cold in Madison during this time, and we worked outdoors on the roof. When you are coming out of Florida, you can only imagine how difficult it was for me to adjust to a northern climate, but I did what needed to be done (with tears and all). At the end of our workdays, he would sometimes prepare a small meal and then drop me off downtown in enough time so I could get in line at the shelter to secure a bed for the night. I can remember there was nights he'd allow me to stay in his basement where there was a bed. I loved it. He allowed me to use his laptop and the privacy versus the shelter. I really needed that. However, at the shelter, they fed us upon arrival, and in the mornings before exiting the shelter, which is where they also housed us. The only thing that really sucked was when we'd be kicked out the housing unit by 7 a.m. in the morning (in my opinion,

The Life That Brightens the Light

this was one of the coldest point of the morning). The cold air was brutal. I can honestly say Grace Episcopal Church, at 116 West Washington Avenue, saved my life. I would have easily died over night trying to sleep outside in Wisconsin. I have no idea what I would have done.

This is me servicing my high profile client in Madison. (Roofing)

The reason I was using Porchlight services due to the fact that my identification wasn't accepted for the clinical trial. Nope! That first initial appointment was rescheduled, and I needed a valid identification. I was in a new city and state, and I had to locate and secure a social security card and a birth certificate in order to get new identification. They mail the identification to you after you finally verify your identity, but I was homeless without an address to receive the identification. I couldn't leave the state without that identification, which is in accordance to the Department of Transportation's laws. Yep, I was officially stuck in Wisconsin. I didn't panic. I did the administrative work to figure it all out. I found the requirements to secure Wisconsin State identification. I located their offices and associated fees. I satisfied all obligations on my end and secured the identification. Porchlight has a service that allows the homeless to use their address to receive mail. Porchlight paid for the identification, but not before doing what they required of me in order to receive the benefit. This entire process took a month and a half.

When I finally received my identification, it didn't take me long to hit the road since the clinical trial was a failure. I departed Madison on November 2, 2015 and headed for Los Angeles, California. I was very disappointed by the previous medical trial, but there was another one in California. I called and scheduled another appointment with a different company.

I boarded the Greyhound not realizing how long this trip would be. It was miserable because every time I drifted into a good sleep, it was time to get off the bus. The layovers were so long that I felt a stolen car was better than the headaches associated with the trip on the bus. Of course, I wouldn't dare, but the thought was enough to help me endure the difficulty a little longer.

The bus was on a layover in Phoenix, Arizona.

The Life That Brightens the Light

We drove through Minnesota, Iowa, New England, Oklahoma, Texas, New Mexico, and Arizona until we finally reached Los Angeles. My eyes couldn't stop scanning my surroundings as we drove because I've been to Cali before, but for business. I'll never forget when I first arrived in L.A. I was so excited to be there. It was so confusing because the morning time in California looks like the evening time on the East coast. I tend to explore a city when I first get into a new city. I was in Los Angeles, so there was so much I wanted to see--and I saw it all! I needed shelter, and I had already done the research on the bus. I was on that bus a day or two, if I am not mistaken. At this point in my life, I had enough experience with homeless shelters to know what to expect. There were a lot of cons, but the pro's existed too. I spent a lot of time on the streets the first few days, but it was very difficult finding a good place to sleep on the street in L.A. I needed to choose an area and a safe place in the area to sleep comfortably. In my opinion, Los Angeles is not a great place to be homeless if you don't have a talent or skill. There was a huge homeless population in L.A, and it was 85% bigger than Madison (in my opinion). Therefore, when I got hungry, it was not as simple as going to a gas station and asking for money, and singing had little effect in producing an income (Panhandling).

Let's side track a little bit.

When it comes to the homeless, please avoid prejudging anyone who approaches you. Of course, you must prejudge as it pertains to safety, but outside of safety try to remove your assumptions and just help if you can and don't if you cannot. Don't assume you know their circumstance or the emotions associated with their situation. Just do your part without anything extra, such as prejudging anyone. With my experience, it is a very depressing situation. I always fought myself from approaching and asking people for change or help. It is NOT a good feeling. It feels horrible emotionally. However, when I met the people who would assist in any way they could without resistance or judgment, it gave me the strength and the confidence to keep going. I felt a little better. Besides, it made life a little easier in my moment of desperation. I didn't do drugs, drink alcohol, throw my money at prostitutes, or whatever else people feared I'd do negatively with what they gave. I never lied about the use for the money or I'd avoid the reason altogether. Do your part because I personally believe the karma involved with this process will come back around to save you when you personally need mercy.

Okay, back to the story!

For years, I simply went to a gas station, grocery store, Wal-Mart, or a convenient location where there is foot traffic and sing for money. My first time panhandling was when I was only 15 years old. This wasn't a complicated task. I would usually have to panhandle for one or two dollars for the bus. When the foot-traffic or exposure to people is low or non-existent, the need is a serious need. So, I'd always make sure before the city slow down I'd be full of food going into the night, and I must have a few dollars for the morning unless I want to work as soon as I awoke. Thank goodness for the shelter because they understood this concept and fed us upon arrival and departure. However, as an adult, the skill of panhandling has bought plenty of pampers, formula for infants, as well as fuel and food on several occasions. It was usually easier when I took my girls with me so people didn't think I was doing it for drugs or whatever they would make up in their heads. I have NEVER been into drinking, smoking, or doing drugs. Once I was in Los Angeles, this skill wasn't effective as the other states.

I remember when I was in Madison, a homeless friend of mine told me about Venice Beach, California. He told me I should go there and sing. He said I would make a lot of money with my voice. I took his suggestion lightly at the time, but as I walked the streets of Los Angeles, this would be a good time to discover the possibility. I decided to scout Venice Beach. Once I figured out how to get there using public transportation, I walked the stroll only to find someone performing every 5 yards for miles. It was incredible because if you had something for sale or if you were seriously talented they would tip you. I sat and watched performers for about a week. Then, I learned about the Santa Monica Pier and the 3rd Street Promenade. It was just as good as Venice Beach if not better. While in Venice Beach, I was given a unique opportunity and it helped a lot with money for transportation and food.

I was at Venice Beach scouting the talent and exploring the area I would potentially be performing in. I took a little break near the basketball court because I loved basketball. While taking a break from walking with all my property, I noticed a kid shooting a basketball. I have been a fundamental basketball trainer of children for years. Every time I see a child working on his/her fundamental skills, I intervene. In this case, I decided to get up and give him some instruction by way of exercises in order to improve his fundamental shooting skills. I worked with him for about 30-45 minutes before his mother approached us with a gentleman at her side. She was curious as to who I was and why I decided to assist her son. Being a concerned parent, I granted her wish and explained my history as a trainer and described my training methods. She was intrigued by my ability and she explained, "I take my son's career in the sport very seriously, and I am very cautious about who is permitted to work with him."

She went on to explain that her cousin stopped her when I initially made an attempt to instruct her son. He wanted her to watch and see what I'd do and how. This young, "beautiful" woman happened to be Lavonna E. of Geffen Records, Interscope Records, and Priority Records, and her cousin worked with the Los Angeles Lakers training camp and had a very prosperous career in his industry. Lavonna's cousin went by the name "Silas White," and he was a business manager, brand consultant, artist manager, and an A&R who has worked with artist like Justin Timberlake, 3x NBA champion Bryon Scott, Brain McKnight and many more. These two are very good friends of mine. They both watched me train her son, Christon, without my knowledge, and again, they were impressed. My experience from the corporate world has taught me to stay on the topic of the engagement. Yes, I was in California to be discovered as a singer, but this was NOT the circumstance to present myself as a possible candidate. I respected them and our relationship. I was open to opportunities, but I would leave the idea up to their discretion on the topic. She definitely was excited about the idea of me possibly training Christon if we could figure out the details.

We made plans, and I began to train Christon for compensation on a weekly basis throughout my time in California. This opportunity opened the door for me to train three of his teammates which led to some income outside of singing and panhandling. This opportunity has saved me on many, many occasions, and I am so thankful for the opportunity to meet every single one of them. At one point, Lavonna and I were discussing the idea of me starting a training camp for children because 1) She believed in my gift to teach and train, 2) She has been rubbed the wrong way with the trainers in her area. She felt Christon had shown a ton of improvement with the little time spent training with me. I wasn't responsible in my role of making the training camp tangible. This is due to the final result of my reason for being in Los Angeles, and I do apologize for my neglect with the given set of circumstances. She understood my position, but she was quite disappointed and rightfully so. However, five-and-a-half years have passed, and I still possess a healthy friendship with all of them. Christon has been accepted into college to play basketball (at the time of the publishing of this book). Getting back to the story.

After seeing people making money, I decided to do a test run. I went out there one day hoping to have a prosperous day. That was NOT the end result. I didn't make one penny. I needed to find a way to make this work. I failed on three consistent days. A bystander suggested I get a public address system (P.A. system) similar to the ones every other performer used out there. Again, I took this tip lightly, but I was desperate for the income on day three of my attempt. It was time to revisit the drawing board. I decided to entertain the idea and began conducting some research on buying a P.A. system. I spent a day or two visiting locations that sold them. They were so easy to find, but I needed about $200. The storeowner identified the P.A. that worked for my circumstance. I told the storeowner I would be back to get it.

I still didn't have any income, and the homeless shelter fed me along with food banks and food drives. It had been almost two weeks that I had been in town. It had never taken this long to create some income on the streets. I knew the little income from training was coming, but it would be a week or so before I generate that. Plus, it wasn't going to be $200. I was determined to figure out the Venice Beach opportunity. In case you didn't know, the goal at this point of my life and since I left Orlando was to force income using my ability to sing, so I could not look for or obtain a legitimate job. The principal I was adopting was "What you focus on expands." You have heard it so much. That simply means if you concentrate all of your efforts on one idea and on one task, the law of attraction will work in your favor and open the doors of opportunity. I knew this force of appreciation using my ability to sing would be easier if I continued to endure the difficulty of focusing all my energy into singing and getting paid for it. The law of attraction has to be applicable at some point. When? I had no idea, but I knew I'd do my part. You'll see what happens. Let's keep going.

So the P.A. system was waiting for me. I needed to make $200 in order to buy the system I needed so I could street perform singing on the beach in order to make some money. It was during the evening in downtown Los Angeles when I inquired about the P.A. system and given the price. I decided I would hunker down for the night and early the next morning, I'd start panhandling--hopefully for the last time-- so I could raise the money and pay for the P.A. system. That was the plan. Remember, this has been one of the worst places in the U.S. to panhandle for money. The overgrown homeless community in L.A. makes it nearly impossible to generate any income from citizens. I was faced with the task of not only hitting my goal, but also having a goal higher than I usually panhandled for. I usually panhandled for an average of $5 - $20 for food and transportation. Tomorrow my goal was to make well over $100, but this was necessary for me to move on to the next step in my mission.

I went back to the shelter, waited in the long line, stored my baggage, checked in, showered, ate, and got some rest among other people in my situation. We were awakened on time the next morning around 5 a.m. I ate and hit the road by 7 a.m. I already knew the area where I was going to begin working. I was out there singing and begging. When I don't feel like singing I just ask for it. It is a horrible feeling. You literally feel like the lowest thing on the planet, begging people for change or whatever they can spare, but it builds character if you allow it to. It took all day, but I did it. I was so happy with myself. When I wanted to give up, I reminded myself of why I was out there and what I would create in the future would be forfeited if I quit.

The closer I got to the goal, the less I cared about the embarrassment and humiliation. Immediately, when I made the last dollar, I was on the next bus to go retrieve my first rechargeable P.A. system. You see having a plan helps you to know what is at stake. A plan will keep you accountable. That plan was the reminder of the big picture, and all these little tasks were a step closer to something bigger. Those small individual tasks were five fingers coming together to create a fist to throw a mighty blow. So you cannot excuse the little things because they are an element to complete the big picture. Think of it like a puzzle. The focus is this: at the beginning you have all these little pieces. When they come together in the correct sequence or order, they create the big image. I knew this because I had a plan and I couldn't quit what I hated because I would say no to my own outcome (The Big Picture/The End Result of My Plan). Again, a plan will keep you accountable. This is another advantage of having a good plan. The confidence, the direction, the steps, and the accountability associated with knowing what is at stake.

I made it to the store before closing and purchased the exact P.A. system the storeowner and I discussed. I walk a few blocks to the bus stop. At the bus stop I could not turn the system on because it required a plug. Disappointed, I headed back to the store. Keep in mind, this entire time I have been carrying two heavy bags everywhere I went all day long since leaving Florida. Now, after leaving the store, I have those bags, and you can add a 90lbs. P.A. system. I have to walk nearly three blocks back with equipment that is useless to me. The storeowner hassled me a little, but my sales background has taught me how to negotiate very well. He ended up feeling bad and giving me a P.A. system that had a higher value than the one I initially bought at no additional cost. That meant this mistake rewarded me something I couldn't afford, and it was much better than the one I took back.

The Life That Brightens the Light

This is a great example why you should NEVER lose your cool when unfavorable circumstances arise. Approach EVERY situation with a positive attitude because I am sure if I had acted like I had no sense, I probably would have been stuck with equipment I couldn't use. Always be in control of your attitude. The energy you put out into the atmosphere matters when using the law of attraction. Be aware of your energy. How do you do this? Well, are you happy, sad, angry, frustrated, upset, mad, or irritated? If you do NOT have positive emotions, the reality doesn't matter and the circumstances don't matter because your environment is affected by your emotions and not by the reality or circumstances. How do you feel? If you are NOT in a positive state of mind, it is safe to say you ARE NOT giving the atmosphere positive vibrations. Therefore, you can expect to expand what you are putting out into the world. Negative people, unfavorable circumstances, pain, and suffering versus if you are positive where you can expect to receive favor, joy, a positive outcome, mercy, and happy engagements.

With that said, NEVER allow your circumstances to dictate your emotions. You can control your emotions. This knowledge has given you the information you need in order to begin taking control. Do you remember when I mentioned that you could approach every situation with three different options? 1) A positive mindset, 2) A negative mindset, 3) Ignore the circumstance altogether! Those are your choices and there is a lot of power in your decisions. This is what matters-- NOT the circumstance. Get excited to face your trials and tribulations. This is why I found the people necessary in order to afford the P.A. system. I attracted the right individuals by maintaining a positive attitude. I approached people excited about my goals and priorities. I was connecting with those who were open to good energy. Have you, personally, given to someone based on how you felt about them? You were searching the realm for the energy you felt and if the energy was good enough for your intuition. This is the law of attraction. It works. Energy is real. Use it to your advantage. You have a choice. Always approach every situation with a positive mindset. Sometimes, people start off with a negative attitude towards my circumstances and me. When I leave positively they change their minds because the guilt of rejecting a positive energy is noticeable and cannot be left unattended.

People even recognize their own negative energy at times. Where light exists the dark must depart because they cannot exist in the same space at the same time. Be the light.

Have you ever noticed when a negative person enters a positive atmosphere the energy is brought down and vice versa? Are you normally the dark or the light? Complaining all the time is a bad energy; it's the darkness. Just as a positive, optimistic person brings light to a dark room, then the negativity gets up and leaves. Yep, I said it. A negative person usually leaves when a super-positive person enters the room bringing the energy up, or they stay and do what is known as, "Hate." Haters exist! Allow your energy, your light to be brighter and stronger. Don't be held captive by it. Avoid friends and family of this nature. It will improve the overall quality of your life. Trust me.

Never forget that good exists in the world at the same time as the bad and the ugly, but you can call more good into your existence with this light illuminated. Be the best version of yourself. Be aware of your energy. Plus, I am sure you can recall my example of getting the car prepared before hitting the road for a long journey. Your toolbox is beginning to load up for your journey. Use everything you have to power your dream. The bigger the dream, the more power you need to run it. Use every tool in preparation. Getting back to the story.

I called into existence all the favor and mercy that could be conjured up at the moment, and that's why I remained calm, cool and collected. Look at the results. Thank you, universe, God, and the law of attraction for the power to choose the light and receive its benefits. I stacked the odds in my favor. Use this power for your own benefit on your journey to success.

Now, I had the P.A. system. I tested it out at the bus stop and it was super loud. I loved it. Now, I could compete with the competition at the beach. No more acapella and people over powering my voice with their P.A. system. In addition, I could actually take karaoke to the streets and engage those who appreciated my talent. What I do at the karaoke bar I can do anywhere. I still didn't realize the opportunity yet. When I sing at the karaoke bars, people are so impressed and their response to my talent is overwhelming in a good way. So this should equal dollar signs

The Life That Brightens the Light

when I take my gift to the beach. At this point, I had no idea what I was in for.

I am going to take a detour. This is the perfect time to fill you in on the strategic approach to singing at the karaoke bars as it pertains to my goal of getting discovered. Simultaneously I was trying to implement the karaoke strategy while figuring out the sleeping situation every night and honoring the requirements necessary to guarantee shelter. I was also working on finding a good karaoke joint to sing at on a nightly basis to hopefully be discovered. I searched for the best venue to perform in Los Angeles to possibly be discovered by a celebrity or someone of importance. This is L.A., so why wouldn't this be a possibility? Besides, I had the law of attraction on my side, right? I am just waiting for the universe to open the doors of opportunity for me at some point!

I found a few places I liked and visited all of them, but one stood out to me. It was Boardwalk 11 Karaoke Bar in Venice Beach, California. Boardwalk also had a few celebrities that have visited there in the past. Snoop Dogg is one for their books along with actor, singer, and comedian Craig "Monte" Robinson, who tends to visit occasionally. I met Craig and he heard me sing at Boardwalk 11 on numerous occasions, but I never approached him with the "Do something for me attitude." Boardwalk 11 was very convenient because a bus route was close enough to go to and from the karaoke bar to Venice Beach to perform. On the nights I was visiting a karaoke bar. I couldn't go to the shelter because check-in time was at 7 p.m. Obviously, that was very early for me as a singer. I would have my night at the karaoke bar and then I'd walk all night or find a restaurant that was open all night long (with both bags in hand along with the P.A.). I would be so sleepy during the day because of the lack of sleep at night. This wasn't sustainable. I needed to figure this out. So, at this point, I had been in L.A. close to two weeks.

I wouldn't go to Boardwalk 11 too often because I wanted to sleep in a bed and get fed. Now, that I had the P.A. system and the day was almost over, I wouldn't be allowed to check in the P.A. system at the shelter so I stayed in the streets that night. I decided it was time to

This is a picture of me outside Boardwalk 11.

figure out a way to change my bagging system. I decided the clothes I had weren't convenient for my situation, so I started conducting some research. I found an army surplus and a local assistance program. They provided food stamps, $200 in emergency money, and a three-day motel stay in the form of a voucher (much better than what Florida offers). The timing couldn't have been better. The only issue to address was I carrying around two heavy bags and a 90lbs. P.A. system everywhere I went, and I disqualified myself for the shelter unless I lost a bag. So, the day after I got the P.A. system, I located the department that was responsible for getting me all the benefits I previously listed. It was so taxing on my energy and speed of travel walking everywhere with that much property. Also, I needed to stay hydrated throughout the day along with the purpose of singing. The downside to this is EVERY FREAKIN' business doesn't have a public bathroom. So, as a homeless person, every time I needed to use the restroom, it was stressful and problematic. This was the worst experience ever, and words cannot express my hate towards this problem. Imagine walking with all of your property, and you have to go number two. You "WALK" blocks to business after business as they are refusing to allow you access to a restroom while you are in the midst of an emergency. I have had plenty of accidents out there. This was a constant battle everyday not to go on myself. If you are in Los Angeles and you see crap in the middle of the sidewalk, it wasn't me. This is the circumstance they put the homeless in--I get it. They shower in your restroom and make a mess, but what is the happy medium? Also, you notice I mentioning the carrying of the bags. I guess we know why the homeless keep a shopping cart. It's just freakin' easier! No, I didn't do the shopping cart nor did I ever eat out of the trash. It was never that bad.

Anyway, I traveled all over the city and jumped through all the hoops to apply, qualify, and receive the benefits I mentioned. This meant I had three days to make this karaoke machine profitable. I created a system that worked for me. I put my belongings in the room and went to the karaoke bar that first night. The next day, I woke up in the room and traveled to Venice Beach with the P.A. I got to the bus stop and sang a little bit. Can you believe a few people stopped their vehicles or turned around and backtracked to my location to give me a tip as I tested the system? It was basically a sound check. I had no idea what a sound check was at the moment. Once at the beach, I stopped at the Starbucks on the beach, downloaded, stored, and tested all my karaoke tracks. Once I was done, I headed down to the strip on the beach to setup and begin my first set ever with a P.A. I ran into another issue. People will fight you over a spot on the strip. I was competing for a spot where these performers had been performing for years. You cannot step on toes or if you choose to do so, be prepared to defend yourself because they are NOT walking away. I spent a large part of the day searching for a comfortable and convenient location to perform. At the end of the day, I found a spot. Well, I cannot call it a spot. It was the bus stop off the beach with little foot traffic. However, I made about $60 that day. I was so excited. It was a full day of walking, but the hour I did get to sing was more profitable than panhandling. Let's just say I was excited for tomorrow. Once the sun was gone I headed to

Boardwalk 11 because I still had the room so it was convenient to travel without the extra baggage.

This is a picture in San Francisco.

I asked if I could place my belongings in a good spot in the venue until I was ready to depart the bar. Guarding property all day all was labor intensive just as walking with it was. I always made sure before I setup to sing at the beach to use the restroom and this is because if I must use the restroom and my stuff is setup for a show will I leave it unattended or pack up everything in order to use the restroom? I am sure you can imagine how much the idea of having to choose would suck. Anyway, due to the fact I still had the room, I didn't have everything I owned with me, yet. The next day, after a great night of singing at Boardwalk 11, it was time to initiate my baggage plan. I threw away all my clothes and everything else that was added weight. I arrived at the military surplus store with the money from the benefit and my little profits from last night, minus the money for food and a soda the previous night at Boardwalk 11. I bought two military style black pants, which possessed utility pockets for extra storage, a military style jacket which had a ton of extra pockets along with a pair of military style steel toed boots. I got a dozen long winter thick socks to go with the purchase and a military style camping backpack that had the potential to carry everything I owned because it had stretchable material. It gets so cold in the desert at night and super hot in the daytime. I wore all my clothes at night when in the elements and had to shed everything during the day. So, now I am down to one bag and a huge speaker. When the room was done, I'd be carrying less property and my attire would help with the outdoors. Everything I bought was water resistant. This was a huge bonus, right? Plus, I was much more comfortable.

Do you notice how I am finding creative ways of making my survival easier? This is how the evolution process works. Smart is making a difficult task simple. Also, you can count on adjusting to unfamiliar circumstances. You learn this way. Now I headed back to the beach to secure a spot to setup again. I found a great spot at the Santa Monica Pier. I was there performing 30-minutes before a law enforcement officer approached me and kindly requested my entertainer permit from the City of Santa Monica which I did not possess. I was given information on the process in order to obtain it and asked to leave. They were nice and gave good instruction as to where they couldn't regulate performers. With that said, I remembered a spot I saw a guy performing when I was scouting the location. He wasn't there performing at that moment. It was outside the area of what the law enforcement officers were able to regulate. I setup and I was exposed to more than 300 people in this spot, and no one bothered me all day.

I made more than $200 for three-hours of singing. I was so shocked. I knew I would make money, but $200? Now, I see the value of my gift paired with the P.A. system and a good location to perform. I made more money in California Street performing than anywhere else around the country. No street performing situation has ever paid this much. I made a minimum of $66 an hour on the streets singing. I found that I could charge my P.A. system between the hours of 7 a.m. and noon, which are times unfavorable to performers at Venice beach strip, Santa Monica Pier, and the 3rd Street Promenade. I was developing a system without really noticing it. Of course, at the end of the shift, I'd catch the bus to Boardwalk 11 and order my favor BBQ chicken wings and a Coca-Cola.

At Boardwalk 11, the entire staff knew me along with their rotating roster of karaoke D.J.'s. I was always sure to buy something every time I visited. Everyone there knew my situation and my story. I never panhandled there nor did I use my circumstance to get anything for free or as a pass NOT to buy something. I only went there to sing, but it wasn't looked upon in a positive way to sit in an establishment for 5-hours and buy NOTHING. I would visit Boardwalk 11 on days I wasn't able to sing because the night was long in the streets, and this shortened those long nights. This became my daily process to wake up, charge my P.A. system at a Starbucks, workout at L.A. Fitness, head down to the pier to sing and then Boardwalk 11. This was going to be the process until I was discovered. I would post my videos people captured of me online to increase my exposure as a singer.

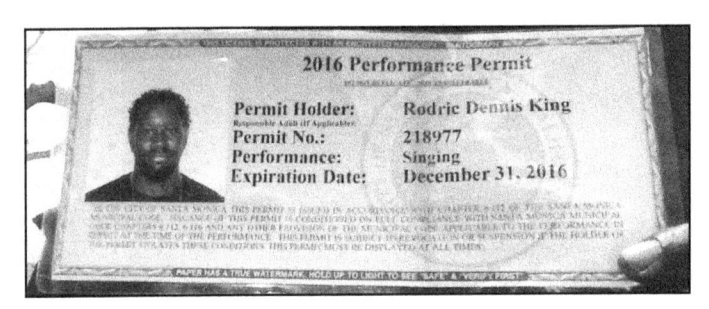

I quickly applied and received my
"Performance Permit" for the city of Santa Monica.

This is a great time to explain another big event that happened while on this singing journey. Due to the fact that I always conducted a ton of research using the laptop I earned while in Madison. I found an audition for the television show "The Voice," but it was across the country in Philadelphia, Pennsylvania. I had no idea how I was going to get from Los Angeles to Philly, which was 3,000 miles away. The window for the audition was very small. The auditions for The Voice had been ongoing but there was only a week remaining for individuals to try out. It was ONLY an opportunity, so I decided that I had nothing to lose by making an attempt to audition in spite of my current circumstances. Besides, I had the perfect story for the show--at least I thought so. I sat back in my seat and began to brainstorm. How could I make this happen? If I do make this audition, I am showing the universe that I am doing everything in my power.

Side Note:

Always keep in mind AT ALL TIMES that you must be proving to the universe that this is something you want. You need to do this not only with your tongue, visualizations and intentions but you must also take extreme action. This event could be considered an extreme act towards my true desire. Therefore, it was in my best interest, as it pertains to the law of attraction, to include this act to amplify the laws in my favor. Was this opportunity going to be the ticket? I had no idea, nor did I care at the time. I don't think or entertain the things that are out of my control. I only do my part and play my role. With this said, you must be on the lookout for opportunities in order to amplify the laws of attraction in your favor.

I tabulated all of my options from the extreme options to the obvious ones. I created a step-by-step plan and took action. I posted on all my social media pages what my intentions were and what I needed from them. No one responded. I hit the streets with flyers and sang at vehicles, gas stations, and everything in between. I was able to earn a few dollars, but I did not hit the goal or come close. I didn't stop there. I continued to pitch my plans to individuals I knew but to no avail.

Then with only a few days left, someone who wished to remain anonymous contacted me privately. This individual stated, "I have a family member who is well off and owes me a few favors. I am suggesting that he cover all of your expenses because I seriously adore and believe in you. Also, I want to see you make it. However, I DO NOT want my doing so advertised or made known. I wish to remain anonymous. Can you honor my wishes?" I quickly agreed to the terms and thanked this person the best I could with the words I could find. As you can imagine, I was so thankful. This person stated, "I am waiting for a reply. As soon as I have an update I will fill you in on the details."

Well, it took a full day and I heard back from him. He found an Airbnb in a nice area in downtown Philly and booked it along with my round trip flights. I gave him the necessary information and before you knew it, I was boarding a plane. This was NOT only a trip, but a bit of relief from my circumstances. I had been living on the streets for months and the break from the lifestyle was amazing. Plus, I had a glimpse of what the celebrity tour life would be like in a few days.

I arrived and got situated in my sleeping quarters. Of course, I explored the city a bit while on a budget because my sponsors gave me a few dollars to cover and absorb food cost as well as local transportation. The next day I located the venue and arrived early. Prepared and anxious to sing my heart out, I am in line being very attentive to the process in place for such an event. There were so many singers. Words cannot describe the turn out. The lines were so long just as the process was for auditioning. We were separated into groups. There were about 10 gigantic rooms, and each room had a producer from the show. There were groups of 20 acts per room. We were standing in front of our room waiting for further instruction, and all of a sudden we were greeted by a producer of the show (this was not a celebrity). He explained what we could expect and the process we were to undergo. Next we were brought inside the room in a single file line. The order we were standing is the order we would perform our audition. It was finally my turn to sing, and I thought I killed it.

A young lady by the name of Kimberly Jo Hale was up, and she sang. I was expecting to lose to her because her vocals were polished and very experienced. Kimberly is a pianist, singer, producer, and music arranger. She is a Dayton, Ohio, native who traveled to Philly to audition like I did. After everyone auditioned, we both realized we didn't make the first round--and we were both confused. I knew she was one of the strongest singers of our group, and she felt I was which I learned during our discussion after the audition. We exchanged information and have been in touch ever since. We have plans to one day collaborate on a project together. The opportunity has yet to present itself.

So, after it was all said and done, I finished my day and made my returning flight back to Los Angeles in disappointment. I wanted to return to give everyone who was routing for me great news. I didn't have that and it felt horrible letting everyone down (there were a ton of locals who wanted a report when I'd return). At that moment, while in flight, I determined I would discontinue the process of auditioning for platforms of this nature. I decided I'd build my own fan base because I have been a marketer for top corporations. Why couldn't I use my knowledge and build my own fan base? This was my mission after completing the "Paid Full-time Singer" objective. Now back to the story!

At this point, it was time to leave the motel with all my property. The process was in place, and by the fourth day of singing at the pier, my voice was completely gone I can't sing. My voice felt damaged and the sound seemed to be permanent damage. Can you imagine the fear? You are traveling the country trying to get discovered as a singer, and your gift is gone forever. I was faced with this tribulation, but it was only a temporary fear. Obviously, my voice came back. It took about three days of vocal rest. I had no idea what vocal rest was until I experienced this issue of NOT having a voice. When professional singers overuse their voice or don't give it rest, it tires out requiring vocal rest. Vocal rest is a couple days of NO PHONATION. No talking, shouting, whispering, or vocal phonation. It's very difficult, but very necessary in order to protect your instrument. In a week, I'd spend about 4 days singing and three days of vocal rest. I wouldn't be able to sing anything by day number 5. I learned to rest my voice. The best day ever was about $400 for a four hour set.

I decided to do research on the vocal issue and I learned how to take care of my instrument. I had no idea what I was being prepared for. You'll soon see why this process was necessary. The good thing is I had some money to hold me over, but I was currently faced with not having a place to sleep. So, I didn't go to Boardwalk 11 since I couldn't sing. I decided to head down to the shelter for those three days. By the second day, I was done with the shelter for good. The time constraints limited what I could do in one day. Check in at 7 p.m. was too early and out by 5 a.m. when it's cold and everything is still closed except for Starbucks and the gym. Plus, the shelter was downtown Los Angeles while my performing area was 45-minutes away. Why did I give up on the homeless shelter? The time constraints was one thing, checking in bags was another risk, but the final straw was having elderly men taking a dump in the showers where we MUST shower before being accepted into the shelter. I couldn't go into that shower knowing people defecated on the floors. So, elder homeless men need assistance because they are elderly. They should be in a nursing home, but their life isn't setup that way. As an individual using the shelters services, I was forced to deal with the issues created or stemming from the causes of the elderly even if they can't get to the toilet quick enough to avoid taking a crap on the shower floors.

I was done. I vowed to never go to another shelter again. I had to find a process for getting sleep in the streets. Spending the money I was making on a roach motel wasn't an option. The worst motel in Florida averages about $40 and here in California the same motel is $85. I prefer to sleep in the elements with a pocket full of money versus trading my hard earned money on an overpriced room. So, I am back at Boardwalk 11 and I can't sing. They are closing for the night and I have nowhere to go. I can't keep trying to get by staying in restaurants that are open 24-hours. I needed to find a comfortable place to sleep. So, Boardwalk 11 is closed. I found a place to sit and think right across the street from the venue. It turned out this is a good spot to sleep on the sidewalk since the neighborhood was safe and free from homeless people or at least it was. I decided to put all my belongings under the picnic table I was sitting at. This table was located outside a restaurant on the sidewalk. I got underneath the table using my belongings as a pillow. This was a tactic to guard my property while I slept.

Now I found my shelter for the next few months. My process every day was to sleep here, wake up, and go charge at Starbucks and workout when I needed a shower. I would sing during the day at the Santa Monica pier when I had a voice, and every night I was at Boardwalk until it eventually closed. During this time, I met a lot of locals. They were spreading the word about this homeless guy that comes and sings every night. People were paying me from time to time to sing their song. It was usually a song out of my arsenal that was one

The Life That Brightens the Light

of the 30 songs I'd street perform during the day at the pier. I was averaging $190 to $220 a day singing at the pier, average. A full day of singing was 2 to 4 hours. I always had a large wad of money from tips. I appeared homeless when I went into a store to make a purchase because of my bags and my attire, but when I pulled out my money the jaws dropped. I could have easily paid for a motel, but it was $85 for the worst motel room ever. Again, I preferred to sleep on a sidewalk with a pocket full of money. I showered every day, but not washing my clothes every day and the persistent sweat due to overheating during the day caused me to smell!

Eventually, my process had come together, and this was my process every day. I had a good friend who was a karaoke DJ at Boardwalk 11 that offered to help me when and where he could. Evan and his wife, Jennifer, both agreed it was okay to sleep at their apartment when I absolutely needed shelter, but a shower was something I could take advantage of when it was convenient for them. I was so grateful for their kind gesture, and I did take advantage of their offer on numerous occasions. I mentioned to them I loved going up into the mountains to hike, and they offered to take me one day. I was excited about that because they took a 30-minute drive to get to their favorite hiking trail. That meant I was able to see the scenes on the way there if we went. Let's move on.

When I became comfortable with making money on a consistent basis singing at the pier, I decided I was going to explore the West Coast because I was familiar with the East Coast but not the West. That was now going to change. I had even decided I was going to save the money required to travel to Egypt and back. I figured, "Why not?" Plus, I started a YouTube channel called "Video Diary of Rodric King." I wanted to get video coverage of everything I was doing, during this time, and I did. You can type "Video Diary of Rodric King" into the search box on the YouTube platform right now. You will see videos of some of the things covered in this book. So, when my voice was gone, I'd conduct a little research and figure out what was the best form of transportation to go from city to city. If you know anything about the West Coast there are competing tour bus companies everywhere in the Los Angeles and Las Vegas areas. I decided to travel to Las Vegas, San

Francisco, and San Diego on the days I couldn't sing. I wanted to see as much of this part of the country as possible. When I arrived in these cities, I figured out the best way to find shelter was the streets or the shelter. One night while I was sleeping underneath the picnic table, I had a dream I was wearing a brand that wasn't familiar but identical to Tommy Hilfiger and Polo. The name of the brand was "John Tears." I thought it was a decent clothing line, and I loved the way I felt wearing it. When I finally woke up to start my day, I was curious about the brand I saw in my dream and decided to do some research while I charged my P.A. system. I wanted to know if this brand existed already. At this point in my life, I have taken some classes in trademark protection. After realizing that John Tears was not a clothing brand in existence, I decided to do the research necessary to see if the name of the clothing line could be protected, and I'd figure out the strength of the protection. I discovered the protection of that name was limited or weak. I figured I'd alter the name a bit in order to protect the brand when it became popular. So, after days of playing around with John Tears, I founded Hon Tiers. It had the same ring to it with a new spelling, and the protection involved with the name was stronger than John Tears. Immediately, I began the process of creating a logo when I was at the Starbucks in the morning charging. I even launched a corporation for an event I would host, but I needed a company to be the host so I could brand the event. I can't share the details of the event in this book, but hopefully as you are reading this, the event has been revealed and currently successful.

At the time, I had a laptop I earned when I was working with my client from Madison. I mentioned a laptop he allowed me to use from time-to-time. Well, I gave him permission to hold back wages to cover the agreed upon sum for the laptop. This laptop has traveled with me everywhere since leaving Madison. This laptop had the Windows operating system, and I used the paint program to create my logo for Hon Tiers from scratch along with the corporation's logo. Then, I spent weeks building the company and trying to decide what the company values were along with its mission statement and company vision. It took a ton of time, energy, and research to figure that out, but I found it. I started studying as much content as I could consume and understand

The Life That Brightens the Light

in order to learn how to build and structure a new line. It wasn't long before I had an idea who and what Hon Tiers was to me. Now, I needed samples, but it came at a cost I couldn't afford at the time. So I continued tweaking the vision, company mission, and the meaning of Hon Tiers.

Hon Tiers Polo Shirts.

After spending so much time, planning, and structuring my future businesses, I continued to stay positive and patient for the opportunity that would provide exactly what I was looking for. I had a strong desire to become a professional singer and get a full-time pay for doing so without having to sing at the pier. Every night as I would lie down to go to sleep, I'd visualize myself on a huge stage with a full band and a large crowd. During the day, I'd watch celebrities and their lives so when I lie down at the end of the day, I could replace them in my vision with myself. I had images that I captured from their day-to-day travel up to arriving at the venue and the crowd screaming after I hit a crazy high note in a song I was performing. I knew if I wanted my dream to come true, I had to picture it with myself in the vision. You usually receive what you dream, and I knew what I'd focus on would expand.

One day while sitting at the picnic table, I received a call from an unknown caller. The number calling wasn't saved in my contacts. I answered every call because you never knew if the opportunity would come through the window, the front door, the back door, or the chimney. I answered the phone, and a lady was on the phone filling me in on her background and what she does. I had received so many opportunity calls of this nature that I didn't really believe anything I was hearing. Therefore, when she recognized my energy, she took several steps back and said, "Okay, from the tone of your voice you don't believe what I am saying, right now. So let's do this. I am going to send you a link to a video so you can visually see what I do. If you like what you see, please feel free to call me back."

I responded, "That actually sounds like a plan." Before we hung up, the phone alerted me with notice of a new notification. I opened the message and she sent the link she promised. I opened it and the video started to play. I saw everything in this video that I visualized every single night. I was only 20-seconds into the video when I began searching for her number to call her back. Let's just say "she had my attention." When she answered I said, "Hello, this is Rodric King, the singer." I could hear the laughter in her voice saying, "Okay, are you ready to talk, now?" I was more than ready.

She said, her name was Krislyn Rojas, and she was the owner of an entertainment company out of Orlando, Florida. Her company had a few bands, and she was in search of a male "Front Man" lead singer. She saw my version of "When A Man Loves A Woman" online and she was interested in seeing if I was a good fit for the open position. Then she asked, "What city and state are you in because I saw you in a video in Orlando, Florida, but had a number out of New York?" I told her I was currently in Los Angeles, California, but I was more than willing to relocate and commit to relocating long-term if the opportunity is a good fit. She asked if I would be willing to fly back to Orlando,

The Life That Brightens the Light

Florida, one way and when would I be ready to do so. I said, "Immediately." She said, "Okay, I'll pay for a one-way ticket to get you here. We'll give you about three or four shows to make sure this is a good fit for both you and me. If it works out, then you'll have a permanent position with our band as the lead singer of Blonde Ambition band. I quickly accepted and all the details were shared with me.

Immediately after the call, I wasn't walking the same. The law of attraction has proven to me that it is real. I wasn't skeptical at all about the opportunity. However, I was a little excited that the opportunity was in the exact same city I left in order to find a full-time singing position. Let me point something out. I was in the same city with this opportunity for years and putting myself out there to possibly become a part of a winning opportunity to sing for a living. There were so many individuals with resumes bigger and stronger than mine, but I got the position while on the opposite end on the country. There were individuals that were applying for the position and still didn't measure up with the application of the law of attraction. This power is real if applied properly and intentionally.

Think about that! I was in Orlando for years, and I even realized later I was singing in venues with members of the entertainment company as the host. I was a ghost. However, only after applying the laws of attraction, the door to the opportunity forced them to find me. The energy you put out, along with the focus, must be detailed and concentrated. What you focus on expands.

I knew what I wanted. I proved to the universe how badly I desired it, and I concentrated all my energy into the principle, "What you focus on expands." I didn't know how it was going to happen or where the opportunity would come from. I didn't care either. I just know what I wanted and what I needed to do in order to get it. I stayed consistent despite anyone's disapproval or disbelief. I continued the path even if my circumstances were unfavorable. I endured no matter what was thrown at me because my mind was made up that this must happen, and I was going to be consistent no matter what. What the universe saw? I was serious, and I wouldn't be deterred. Therefore the universe had to open the doors of opportunity and move the right things in the universe to give me EXACTLY what I desired all the way down to the specifics. This is why you MUST know exactly what you want. Everything I was getting was in my vision and lacking nothing in comparison to my vision. I created exactly what I intended to create using the tools given in this book. You can do this too.

Understand you cannot call your desire, the dream, because the dream is literally putting yourself in a trance or a hypnotic state and intentionally visualizing what you want. This cannot be possible if you have no idea what you want. It must be crystal clear in your mind's eye. When the vision isn't clear, get some help by finding visuals of what you should be visualizing. As an example of this, I'd go to YouTube and search for videos of celebrities singing at their shows. Before going to sleep every night, I'd replace the celebrity with me in the exact same vision and picture myself in their place. Every chance I'd get, I'd watch more videos in order to fine-tune my visions. I'd try to do this for hours. Literally, a few weeks of doing this I received the call. I made the visions before bed a habit. It felt good living in the vision. Today, this is my reality.

When you actually live the dream and make it a reality, the experience isn't foreign. However, it can be an emotional experience when these events are tangible. At this point, the ticket from L.A. to Orlando had been purchased and confirmed. I would leave in three or four days and I told everyone that my journey is over. The locals in Venice Beach area adjacent to Boardwalk were so excited for me. They all chose days to come out and hear me sing live before flying back to Florida. My good friend and his wife wanted to make sure I had the ability to go hiking with them in the mountains before my departure date. So we hit the trail a day before I officially left Los Angeles. It was a wonderful experience. The entertainment company assisted with locating shelter in Orlando and helped me with the transportation from the airport to what I'd soon call home.

In order to become a full-time singer with Blonde Ambition, I was given the task of learning 20-30 songs in two weeks and I had to be prepared to perform these songs live with the band in only two weeks without lyrics onstage. Let's examine this a little bit.

At this point in my life I had been singing at karaoke's all over the country for the past 5 years. What does this mean? Well, if you know anything about karaoke, the lyrics and the timing of the lyrics are on screen in front of the individual singing. I have been accustomed to singing with lyrics on a screen for years. I've never had to memorize lyrics. Even in the event that I knew the lyrics I was super dependent on those lyrics on the screen. Now, for my circumstance, I had the opportunity of a lifetime, and I am faced with a big challenge. What's the challenge? Well, I've gone my entire life saying aloud, "I have a horrible memory." Guess what? This thought has to be deleted and rescinded because my new career depends on the success of eliminating this mental block. This thought, idea, or concept has held me back for years. Now that I understood how the mind works, I needed to address this subconscious thought because I knew it was self-sabotaging. I had to visit the soil in my mind again. Of course I was going to learn how to memorize lyrics, but before I really took this seriously, I had to overcome the mental challenge I have shaped and developed over the past 23 years. These thoughts are no longer serving me. That was the first challenge. The second challenge was performing with a live band. In reality, I have no live band experience, so I needed to adjust very quickly.

I soon learned that the music sounds different from a track playing. I had a fear of losing my place in the song where the lyrics should be sung. The compounding effect of these elements made the task that much more daunting. We had rehearsals, but it still was not for a live audience, which led me to the next challenge. Could I sing these songs and overcome the challenges of my memory and the music sounding different? Could I perform for a live audience with the number in attendance much greater than a typical karaoke night? It wasn't like I was singing one new song with lyrics I needed to learn. It was more like a catalog, but this was the fence between the circumstances I am leaving behind in L.A. and the new opportunity that I've desired for years and dreamed of every night for weeks.

I reprogrammed my thinking (I dug up the old seeds and planted new ones for a different harvest) and began taking the appropriate steps to begin learning all the songs I was expected to sing and perform. I would listen to these songs all day and all nightlong. I literally tortured myself for the entire two weeks to drill these songs into my head. When I was sleeping, these songs were playing on repeat because I wanted to maximize my exposure to them. Why wouldn't I when I knew what was at stake? This opportunity wasn't going to fade to black because I couldn't hold myself accountable. Besides, this entertainment company and its owners were giving me a chance while taking a chance themselves. I wasn't going to let them down. I had their best interest in mind along with my own. Krislyn and Luis Rojas - is part owner, music director, and bass player for their company) made this process seamless. I nailed it. It was executed to perfection for them, but it wasn't up to my own standard. I looked at it as surviving another show. I knew I just needed to continue to show progress at every new show, and this has been my mentality until this day. I am grateful for them for giving me an opportunity. I couldn't dance for anything, and it's a part of the job description. I eventually caught on. I moved better on stage than when I started.

Keep this in mind--when your day comes to award what you desire, there will be challenges. If you aren't mentally prepared for the challenge, the dream could be lost. I have no idea how often the door of opportunity would open, but get yourself ready for the day your dream becomes tangible. I have no idea what your challenges will be, but you should have an idea. Even if you do not, be open to take on whatever is thrown your direction. You will know exactly what's on the line when the opportunity presents itself to you. Be prepared to take on a challenge. Prove yourself to yourself.

When you are faced with any challenge, treat these circumstances as an exercise before the big game. All the challenges I took on while in the streets of L.A. prepared me for the day when my life changing experience came along. My success on this new level depended on my mental ability to take a challenge and be a warrior. You get to choose your approach. You have three options. You know the options so choose wisely. That is the story of how I became a professional singer.

Let's move on to the next chapter covering "The Extreme Power Concept" so you can get the right information in order to change some of the seeds in your soil. We are about to equip you with everything you'll need to receive the harvest you deserve. Plus, you'll better understand these concepts I've applied to get the results I currently have.

Chapter 4

Extreme Power Concept

"What Is the Extreme Power Concept?"

Now, let's begin to reveal the contents of this book.

The Extreme Power concept is a concept I discovered and applied to my own success. There could be another name for this, but if there is I am unaware. This is the first step to obtain control of your reality using the extreme power concept. This is portion of the book slightly touches the mental side of this new venture you will explore. It is in my opinion, as individuals, we have lost control over our reality so let's turn this around by starting with the basics.

Keep in mind this is an idea or concept. However, I have a strong belief that this idea can and will make a huge impact on the life you are leading as it did for my own life. Let's dig in!

Reality can be defined as *the world or the state of things as they actually exist, as opposed to an idealistic or notional idea of them.* In my own opinion, I've found that there are a lot of people living life by default. Think about that! Living your life by default.

This is the adoption of pre-selected options, styles, trends, fashion, lifestyle, standards, a belief system, way of life, ideas, and concepts. We are usually conditioned to live like this meaning by being exposed to or spending time out of our lives around something or any one thing or a specific understanding could influence our decisions. With this said, we are simply not in control of our life if we are living according to these beliefs. We are controlled or restricted in our minds, and it is normal that most people do not think past commonality. As a matter of fact, you are considered crazy when you do things out of the ordinary.

Why isn't it okay to be different in society? It should be accepted because we are all different. Well, if we are truly individuals, we should be different, right?

Most people are living without contradicting various ideas about their personal existence. What do I mean? Well, do you accept a common lifestyle, idea, concept, a standard, or your reality as it is? Are you exploring all of the possibilities of life while contradicting different features, ideas, or concepts of your existence? I personally believe you should be in control of the concepts and ideas you accept by scrutinizing them and being aware of what you are influenced by including what you believe to be true or accept as truth--and then consciously apply it to your very nature. Don't fall for anything. If you do fall for it, you must have already determined why it is okay to do so.

Look at it this way. Are you contriving ideas, products, titles, and implementing them into society, or are you the one accepting and declining everyone else's ideas, products, titles, propaganda, movies, and content? Someone or something is creating the trends, the titles, the products and services, ideas, concepts, standards and belief systems we consume and fall in love with. We are constantly being sold or solicited many different ideas, concepts, religions, standards, trends and products. We are told what is normal and what isn't, and we stay on this line and judge those who are different. We are convinced that the standard is the standard and there is no other way of doing things. This is the wrong approach. This is the wrong mentality. We are individuals. We are supposed to be different. We aren't all going to do things the same way. In my opinion, society doesn't support differences. This book is contradicting that idea.

Are you being creative and insinuating that your product, service, idea, concept, trend, and belief system is the best one in the world?

Michael Jordan was a famous basketball player, but had everyone convinced in the 90's that his shoe was the best shoe ever. Regardless of how NIKE convinced America that his shoe was the best thing to hit the shelves, he made more money selling his shoes in one year (2014 - $100-million) than he made during the 15 years playing professional basketball (15-year career - $94-million). Is that awesome or what? We (as a society) were convinced wearing his shoe was a status symbol. That's a strong brand.

The point is this:

What you believe influences your life and what you can or cannot create or make into a reality. A great example is this:

When I started with the Blonde Ambition band, I decided I would conduct research to find the best investment vehicle to create passive income. As I found the investment vehicle I wanted to take advantage of, I realized in my studies that apartment complexes range from $500,000 to upwards of one hundred million. Did I have that type of capital? Not at all. However, I learned there is no shortage of money in the world (where did I get this mindset). In other words, it doesn't have to be my money to acquire an apartment complex (OPM – Other People's Money). Ask an average person about buying an apartment complex, and he will tell you, "I cannot afford food this week, and you are asking me to invest into an apartment complex for financial gains?" The average person doesn't believe he can start investing in an industry with the cost associated with such an asset because he DOES NOT have a millionaire mindset. Guess what? He is right! He cannot afford to invest into that industry. However, if he believes he can, he is STILL correct. What he believed is the truth. Period. Always remember, with a strategic plan you can discover the, "How" of any goal or priority.

The point is this:

What you believe is true because your thoughts, energy, effort, beliefs, and the actions you take create your reality. If you don't change your mind set about the topic, you cannot remove any potential mental blocks or break the self-sabotaging acts against your desire--if it's even a desire you have. Just wait until we touch on the subconscious mind. In other words, you cannot have what you don't think you can obtain.

You wouldn't take the necessary actions in order to acquire it, would you?

An individual that doesn't believe he can win the lottery will not play the lottery. He won't give money to an idea that is considered too risky because he cannot expect a return. Why would he? However, those that want to explore their odds are somewhat optimistic about their chances. So, they play, right?

Let's get back to the Extreme Power concept.

In this day and time, we are so receptive to random titles, standards, ideas, concepts, and groups regardless of their relevance to us and our priorities and plans. Who are you as an individual? Have you ever figured that out? When we were young, we all wanted to fit in, right?

Think about that! Most children want to be accepted. They want to be cool. They labor for a title. They labor to fit in somewhere. This happens before they ever figure out who they are for themselves. Do we not find ourselves searching for an idea of who we are until we are grownups? This should have been discovered as a child, but environmental influences, along with many other distractions, distracted us from discovering who we are as individuals. We also may lack the proper guidance.

Moving forward in this journey, you will wear multiple titles, but you must regulate these titles and characteristics you accept. We will dig into that as you read along. Let's start in that direction.

Are you conditioned? How often do you go to a restaurant and see the menu says, "*Hamburger - $2.29?*"

When you get to the cash register, the total is not the listed price. You never get the cost upfront. Why are you conditioned to accept this? The deal at McDonalds is, "*2 items for $2.*"

When I get to the register and the price is more than $2, I give them problems. I am NOT conditioned to think like that. I question everything. Guess what their response is?

"Well, sir, everyone knows that you must pay taxes." Then, I always ask them, *"Okay, so what is the tax rate?"* They never know. Think about the concept of that conditioning. You are told something false on a daily basis and you accept it. It is a small issue, but big in terms of conditioning. It's an exercise of conditioning. You play this conditioning game everyday making it easier for you to accept things as they are without contradicting it. Practice exercising your ability to question everything.

"THE ONLY POINT IS THE CONDITIONING."

I asked a cashier one day, "Would you please reduce the price of the product I am purchasing and force the cost to be what is advertised?" Meaning, if the cost says "$2.29," reduce the initial cost so when the tax is applied it equals your initial cost or less? She couldn't do that. So, basically, the price ISN'T $2.29, right? The price is $2.29 plus tax.

The point is to question everything. Do not just accept everything. Why are things the way they are, and then decide if that's the game you want to play.

Recap:

Are you contriving ideas, products, titles, and implementing them into society, or are you the one accepting and declining everyone else's ideas, products, titles, propaganda, movies, and content? Someone or something is creating the trends, the titles, the products and services, ideas, concepts, standards and belief systems we consume and fall in love with. We are constantly being sold or solicited many different ideas, concepts, religions, standards, trends and products. We are told what is normal and what isn't, and we stay on this line and judge those who are different. We are convinced that the standard is the standard, and there is no other way of doing things. This is the wrong approach.

This is the wrong mentality. We are individuals. We are supposed to be different.

Meditate on this:

You cannot change anything about yourself without mentally contradicting the emotions, feelings, ideas, thoughts, concepts, and your reality first. This change happens on a subconscious level (digging into the soil which in this case, this is your mind). *"Why do you suppose people usually hit rock bottom before making aggressive changes in their life? Why do you suppose something impactful happens before that major change takes affect? Those changes stick because it's no longer a conscious decision to change. You can consciously forget because you are human and humans forget."* The subconscious mind walls the conscious mind, but more on that later.

Who are you?

I said earlier, *"Most children want to be accepted."* I must give you my interpretation of *"how we get introduced to ourselves,"* or the lack thereof. I am going to dive a little deeper into this subject.

When we are children, we are not taught about ourselves. If you were taught about yourself it's not common. As children, we just want to fit in with something or someone. We'll do what is required to be accepted. That's our introduction to us as an individual. Basically, we never get introduced to ourselves. So, what actually happens then?

Well, we go through the identity crisis. We have no idea who we are as children or teens. When we are different, we are excluded (*or our entire group of people that are similar are excluded*). Most teens know how to fit in, and they do what they need to do to fit in or do what they need to do to stay cool even if it's against who they'd like to be because they don't have an identity, yet. Then, you have the talented and popular teens that protect their reputations and the teens that follow the talented and popular kids, right?

Where in this experience are they learning who they are as an individual? I must admit, what they are learning about themselves are usually lies. However, those that learn who they are and get these lessons are special—and *not in a bad way*. They are rare. I was just that. I didn't follow trends, and I did what I felt like doing. I hated peer-pressure, and I didn't respond well to it. People followed me because I was talented.

Let's just say we convert from a child to teen with no identity yet. As adults, we never spend time creating our identity because we are busy conforming to others. We follow every trend. We watch what is popular. We wear what is popular. When you go against that grain you are labeled crazy or weird, and it's uncomfortable. I always went against trends because I know I am an individual. I like what I like and I don't like what I don't like at the cost of being different or unacceptable in the eyes of my peers. This should be okay in society, but it's not. There is a ton of negative reinforcement about being you. There is nothing wrong with being different. Also, we are too busy as adults with family, kids, work, the bills and everything in between so we can't really look at ourselves. We have this feeling of keeping up with society or the life we are confronted with. We don't have time to learn who we are. Plus, whatever we conformed to while developing into an adult is who we are at the time (the fake version of ourselves). This is why we feel like we deserve more or we are just out of harmony with whom we are or who we are supposed to be.

This feeling is deep down inside. You may even find yourself saying, "I don't know who I am or who I am becoming." So, who are you now? What process did you encounter? Are you living a lie or are you staying true to yourself and filtering out those who are NOT accepting who you are? This will lead to peace and harmony. I don't have all the answers, but I know the freedom I feel being myself. Am I perfect? I know this--I am always becoming a better version of myself than I was the day before. That's the power in a decision. I get to decide. You get to decide. Who are you or who do you want to become. Keep reading!

I met myself, but it started with asking tough questions. What do I like? I disconnected from what society, social media, television, family, friends, clubs, and groups conditioned me to accept as my reality. I control that now. You can like something because you were conditioned to like it *with or without your knowledge*. Is it possible that you have adopted traits, thoughts, concepts, beliefs, habits or anything that is NOT something you personally scrutinized, accepted, and adopted? You tell yourself, "*It's just normal. Everyone in my family does it. It's our tradition. Why would I go against the grain? Why would I do it any other way?*" I don't know, but maybe because you have the power and the authority to decide. What is best for me? Will this help me get where I am going? Do I know where I am going or just floating around with the changing winds?

You may have learned the history of your tradition and never questioned why anyone in your family keeps the tradition. You might ask your parents why they follow certain traditions only to learn they do it because their parents did it. In most cases, they never learn the history or never validated the story. Who is the originator of the tradition? What was their purpose for the concept? Has this tradition evolved into something else? What kind of person was the originator? How have times changed and it's applicability? You may end up recreating the tradition, and in turn, create a new way or trend. That's the point: to become a creator. You may not even agree with the original reason for the tradition in the first place.

This is the first step to having an idea of who I was and who I was deciding to be. It is my duty to inform you that you can be anyone or anything. You must decide what it is you wish to become. Stop following standards by default and take control. You have the right and the authority as an individual to do things differently. That's your right! When I started the process of getting to know myself, I couldn't do that without redefining myself. Yes, redefining myself. What does that mean?

I stripped every title, label, and characteristic away from my identity. I cleaned my slate. How are you going to "know who you are" if you are living according to someone else's standards? And how are you going to "know who you are" if you are living according to someone else's standards and you don't know you are living according

Rodric D. King

to someone else's standards? You could easily think they are your OWN thoughts. Do not be deceived. You could easily think you have already scrutinized these ideas and concepts that you have unknowingly, personally, accepted, but you have not. That's where subconscious programming comes into play, but more on that topic later. Why not live according to your own standards for your own personal reasons?

I have the authority to determine that I wasn't a human. I wasn't black. I wasn't a colored man. I wasn't a man. I wasn't a foster child. I wasn't a student. I don't have to accept any title that is in existence or that is commonly known in society. I learned a title doesn't define who I am. I do. That was very powerful. I can be anyone. Literally. Besides, most of these terms and labels were for communication purposes, anyway. You have the same authority. Exercise it.

Let me say that again:

The majority of all these titles, labels, classifications, groups, names, and identities are for communication purposes ONLY.

You can be ANYONE! Take a pick. You can change as you see fit. Who is hurt or destroyed by your deciding to be someone else? You can change who you are without announcing this to the world. If you are known to be ignorant, you can change that. You can be formally known as the ignorant one. You must know you have that authority. You can literally be anyone today, tomorrow or next year. That is exactly why I am NOT quick to connect with old friends. Who have they become? Is it good or bad? So, who are you going to decide to be? I decided to be a singer in 2009 with little to no experience as a singer. I didn't sing my entire life before this decision. I couldn't even sing. I had to learn, but there is power in deciding who you want to become. With time you can become anyone. Redefine the words in your vocabulary for your benefit.

Example: Definition

Perfect – make something completely free from faults or defects or as close to such a condition as possible.

This is the definition for the word "perfect" that is commonly known in society. That is the general definition for the word, "perfect." Well, I don't like the definition. I decided I would redefine the word.

Perfect – an individual is considered complete when any living being consciously decides he or she is complete (nothing more or nothing less)

This new definition of perfect is NOT commonly known as the official definition in society, and you don't have to share your new understanding of this word with the world. However, if it gives you the permission to pursue your wildest dreams, it can't hurt. How will this simple alteration of the definition give you the permission and confidence to pursue your wildest dreams? I'll be the example.

This definition puts the power of being considered "perfect" in my control. I can finally be perfect. I like this new definition of perfect more than the one society knows and understands. Now, I appear boastful to everyone with the knowledge and understanding of the common definition of the word perfect, right? So, what? Who freakin' cares? I'll control my boastfulness. However, I'm going to confidently pursue the ideas I once deemed impossible for ME because I am perfect. I can't lose.

"I, Rodric King, am perfect. I will walk into this meeting and do my best. I will walk in this room with the confidence required to simply be me and sell myself. I can do this because I am perfect and I deserve the benefits I WILL receive out of the positive results I'll create with this meeting."

I might create a new trend. The possibility exists with the new mindset. It wouldn't be possible if I stayed inside the box of what society knows and understands as the definition of "perfect."

I may NOT be perfect according to the general definition, but I am perfect according to my own understanding. Which one matters the most? The definition that fills you with confidence and control or the definition with all the limiting belief? You see all the things in the world that were once impossible aren't impossible at all. Now, your mind is the limit and not the sky, but you set your mind to a higher limit.

Think about that! The idea that I am perfect is giving me the confidence to accomplish tasks I normally wouldn't even attempt. How is it that? Something as simple as redefining words in my mind has changed my self-image, self-esteem, and my overall outcome. This is the impact that your mindset, mentality, and your decisions have on you every day. This is the secret impact of titles and the acceptance of them. Scrutinize everything anyone every called you and denounce all of them. The titles you keep can be redefined.

Would you be willing to redefine words in your vocabulary to improve your quality of life? Remember, our language is for communication purposes only. You need to be understood, and you need to understand others communicating to and with you. So, who gets hurt when you choose to redefine words for your personal experience as an individual? Nobody! If someone is getting hurt, simply evaluate what's taking place and make the necessary adjustments without losing your confidence.

Remember, I said, "Every day I will labor to be a better person than I was yesterday." I said, "I am perfect and I will control the boastfulness I exhibit." Do the work.

Can you begin to see why successful individuals usually have a significant amount of confidence and self-awareness? They literally define themselves. They know who they are because they are recreating themselves and reminding themselves who they are and whom they are becoming every single day. They walk in the spirit of self and the strength contained in it.

Let's touch on "Success."

Our society shouldn't give us the standard and define success for us because we are all different. We do that! What is success to you? I'll pick this up later.

I teach my children to discover who they are so they can get to know themselves as children. I force them to question everything. Why? I want them to decide how valuable things are to them. They should have the ability to personally scrutinize, accept, and adopt their own beliefs, principals, ideas, and concepts. Yes, we guide and influence that, but overall help them to discover the best version of themselves. I encourage them to like and follow things and people for the right reasons (their reasons). I encourage them to question everything. I encourage them to NEVER stop learning because they need to know how to find the answers to their own questions. I encourage them to NEVER take someone's word for it.

I refuse to stand by and NOT show my children how to discover themselves as individuals. I have often asked my kids throughout their entire childhood, "Who are you?" My hope is by the time they are adults, they are already walking in the spirit of self with knowledge of who they are and who they are deciding to be. When you are true to yourself, you will find yourself surrounded by the right people and attracting like-minded individuals. What you focus on expands. Be aware of being someone you are not--you will attract the wrong crowd. You might find yourself feeling incomplete. Rightfully so.

This next topic was the pivot point in my life.

Titles. Titles are very powerful. Think about this! Here is an idea!

Who on earth labeled you and me "humans?" The answer is obvious--"HUMANS!" We named ourselves humans. Human was first recorded in the mid-13th century from the Middle French *humain* "of or belonging to man." It stems from the Latin word *humanus*, thought to be a hybrid relative of *homo*, meaning "man," and *humus*, meaning "earth." So, a human is not a cow, or a spirit guide, but it is a man coming from and rooted to the earth.

Who determines who I am? Who classified my existence? Why do we take these titles so literal? Let me explain my understanding:

Today, the term "human" is safe to use for communication purposes, but this classification doesn't define who I am as an individual. When I am in conversation-- and I literally need to use common terms amongst the individual I am communicating with--is when this is useful and meaningful. That's as far as it goes.

The internal portion of me, whom I manipulate, is my own while I exist, right? How much do you know about the person who has given you and me this title? What is that persons' name? Where did they live? What influenced them to call us a human? How did they arrive at the term "homo" and "humus?" Sometimes purpose can get lost in evolution. The point is I define who I am, and I have the right to contradict anything. I'm free. Are you not free?

Do you have the power and authority to decide within yourself who and what you are? What are the consequences of doing so? Are there any benefits to questioning this and making a change in our belief system? You need to think about this personally.

What do people think of you? What do you think of you? How is your self-talk? Is your self-talk healthy or not?

I hear people doing things out of order and calling themselves dumb or stupid. What? What are you speaking into existence? What do you believe? Why would you use your unique gift against yourself? Then, you wonder why you receive the wrong end of the stick. Even if you don't believe the positive things you say about yourself, say them. Speak from your heart. If you love yourself and care for your own well-being, you should be speaking good things of yourself and about yourself.

Let's discuss contradicting your reality a little.

Example: Let's say I own a two-bedroom house, but I desire a one bedroom with lots of space. The original owners of the house had a vision for a two bedroom, and that's what they built. I have all of my belongings in one room, and this makes me uncomfortable. Could I put some of my belongings in the other room? Of course, but this is not something I am interested in doing.

The Life That Brightens the Light

One day, I was engulfed with confidence and decided to contradict the initial two-bedroom vision the previous owners had. I decided to reconstruct the floor plan and did what was necessary to legally change it. The wall separating the two rooms disappeared and the adjustment was the ultimate decision. This provided the space I desired and from that one contradiction; it was obvious the house had more potential as one bedroom.

The change immediately gave my reality some benefits. It was what I desired—it was more spacious, convenient, and it opened the door to its true potential. Moving out would have been leaving the situation which is not the same as contradicting it. If I'd never contradicted the existence of the two bedrooms, I would've never discovered the true potential of the house.

The point I want to drive home here is *that you must open your mind to contradicting different aspects of your existence because you don't want to be confined or limited. You may discover you have more potential than what you are currently offering in your current situation with the "invisible leash" off. Hint, hint, the leash is invisible.*

These limiting beliefs can be rescinded. Do what's best for you and your future.

Getting back on track.

Who labeled you and me "humans?" The answer is obvious—"HUMANS!" We named ourselves humans.

Here is another example:

Let's say two Americans own a dog. Does this dog know it's a "dog?" Can this dog spell "dog?" Can it read and recognize the word "dog?" Can this dog pronounce the word? Can this dog confirm it's a dog? Did the "Dog Gods" come out of the sky and classify the identity of our domesticated carnivorous mammal and called it a "dog?" No, no, and no.

This is "Peanut!" He is taken ladies.

Let's say for the sake of the example the dog knows it's a dog. These Americans can no longer support a dog and sells the dog to a Chinese couple on their way home to China. The new owners speak their native language, and now the dog is a Gǒu or 狗.

That means dog in Chinese, but is the dog familiar with this change? No, no, and no.

The dog has no idea that his identity changed with his ownership because of the term used to describe him.

What is the point? The point is this--humans named the dog a dog. This doesn't make the dog a dog. It's just a name, title, or classification for communication purposes, right? Plus, the dog doesn't have any knowledge that it is classified as a dog. In the dog's mind, it just exists in its reality. How does this apply to you and me?

Words have no meaning to dogs. Please don't get into the merits of dogs understanding words or commands. That would be entering the topic of stimulus reaction and when you know how the brain works you can manipulate anyone, including dogs. Words have a meaning to you and me. If I called you doctor, professor, marine, officer, employee, black, white, boy, women, hustler, author, rich, poor, cute, ugly, sick, or stink, you would know the standards, expectations, and the criteria to be considered any of these titles or classifications.

This is true with the title, classification, identification, recognition, name, label, and categorization of the word or term "human." It is my opinion that is natural when you accept the title, immediately your subconscious mind understands the nature, standards, and the expectations of being a human. The word takes a life of its own in your subconscious mind (which has more power) and applies the very nature of its meaning to you, your life, your emotions, your feelings, and your reality. Why not? You accepted it. You believe it. Therefore, it is true. We give it life and space in our reality.

Scenario #1

A guy that you do not know is sitting in a chair. I say to you, "This guy is a doctor." With this title, you can safely determine a few things such as income, lifestyle, education, and industry. You know he drives a nice car. Would you find yourself guessing if he lives with his mom? It is likely that he has his own place. You can guess (in 2021) he makes at least, $160,000+ a year. He probably travels, read a lot, and is highly educated along with many other assumptions.

The point is, with a title there are characteristics that come with the title. If we determined he was a police officer, but at the time he has on plain clothes, we know he is likely to have a weapon and has some tactical training along with basic hand-to-hand combat, communication, and de-escalation skills. We would even assume he is well rehearsed in law.

Subconsciously, we are familiar with the expectations, attributes, and the characteristics of titles, classifications, and most common names and terms. We habitually prejudge people knowingly and without knowingly we are doing so. A title or label helps us to arrive at a determination of who and what a person is or isn't and what they are or are not capable of. Titles can seem very innocent. This is the power of titles. They should be used properly and to your advantage.

This book is showing you that titles should be used for communication purposes only. When you speak you want to be understood, right? We allow ourselves to conform to these titles all too well. I believe on a subconscious level when we accept a title, we subconsciously program and wire ourselves according to the expectation of the titles to our subconscious and our subconscious goes to work to keep us true to the nature of the title. We become the title, behaviorally. The program that makes this happen is called "The Subconscious Mind."

Obviously, there are many cases where people perform under the description of a title and don't like to be called the label they are acting out. We are not talking about that. We all know that exist. Use this information where it benefits you, your goals, existence, and your well-being.

We know the expectation of these titles without thinking about it. These titles are affiliated with descriptions, limitations, benefits, and disadvantages. They are not as simple as a title. In my opinion, our mind uses these titles more powerfully than what we think. Don't underestimate the power of titles or our minds. I want you to be conscious about that. Use this to your benefit. How do you see yourself? Who do you really want to be in a creation mindset? Create the real you.

You may or may not have been taught to be an individual. Read that until it clicks.

In order to know who you are, you must remove all the names, titles, and labels that friends, family, your environment, and society has placed on you. You must redefine yourself. It is time to be who you are deciding to be both consciously and subconsciously.

So, if you've never determined who you are or who you are about to be who have you been? Read that again! Whom have you strived to be if you never decided who you are? It is possible you have been living without purpose or with a false purpose for as long as you've been alive? You have learned how to fit in everywhere. That's fake. You have attracted fake. How? What you focus on expands. You are what you surround yourself with.

Example:

I wasn't always a professional singer. I had to become a professional. In 2009, I started out as a self-taught singer singing in karaoke bars which is a lower level skill as a singer. I started out as a beginner, but with enough time I excelled through the experience levels and eventually capped out. After I leveled up, my talent was discovered and this brought me to a totally different level in my industry by 2016. I began singing professionally with a professional band. I was a beginner all over again, but on a higher level. I learned from some many different examples in my industry and began implementing the things I was learning. Why? The reason is because I was surrounded by advanced performers and you know the saying, "Birds of a feather flock together." Before I knew it, fast-forward 5 years later to 2021, and I am experienced on a professional level. Everyone I had access to was responsible for my advancement on this professional level. This wouldn't have been possible without being surrounded by the talent I encountered on this new level. You are what you surround yourself with.

The point is this:

The affiliation I had with a professional band gave me access to individuals with experience I didn't have. I learned from these individuals by being present. I practiced the application of what I was learning from them and perfecting it. Today, I am a professional due to this experience. Surround yourself with those you want to be like most definitely if you want similar results.

Getting back on track. Titles.

The remnants of all those titles can confuse who you are. You have to many filters. When you are out of harmony with yourself, the feeling of wanting or desiring more can be overwhelming. You may be feeling that you are more or more awaits you.

You are simply out of harmony with yourself. Kindly step out of someone else's standards and discover your own. Walk in the spirit of self. YOUR SELF!

You had no idea who you were or you currently still do not know who you are. That is fine because it is NOT too late. With all the lessons you've learned and all the strife you've endured, it probably gave you a purpose. So, all is NOT lost.

Does it make sense why a person who doesn't know who he or she is could lose confidence and believe the naysayers when talking down about their goals? They cannot stand up for themselves without knowing who they are and the power they possess. Does it sound like I am describing a Disney movie? Think about this!

Notice the characters in Disney movies are always weak before they are aware of themselves? What type of confidence do they display after they know their identity? What type of life do they have before and after that point? Pick a Disney movie and watch how the movie unfolds according to this idea. This is life!

Who are you? Who do you want to be? Who were you trying to be? I have no idea if you are grasping this point, but it is an important concept to understand. You are the character in the Disney movie right now. You need to realize who you are. Reflect on your own life and past circumstances. Who will you decide to be? You can be anyone or anything. You can do a complete 180 and have a different life today.

Now, let's go back to the topic. When you accept the title of a human being you subconsciously accept the characteristics of the human nature. When you accept any title, you subconsciously accept the characteristics of the title. What is the problem with accepting the "human nature" one?

In my opinion, the human nature has restrictions and you subconsciously accept the restrictions of the human nature along with the title. It weakens the confidence we have in our abilities as individuals. I must repeat that:

IT WEAKENS THE CONFIDENCE WE HAVE IN OUR ABILITIES AS INDIVIDUALS.

I think it's time for another example.

Example:

The human nature does not permit a human being to fly without support. You must have something supporting your stability in mid-air in order to be considered in-flight or flying. You cannot, under your own will, sustain yourself in mid-air WITHOUT support from a source, but what if you did?

If you did fly in that manner, it would draw attention from everyone in the world because this isn't normal. It breaks the rules of our human nature. HUMANS CANNOT FLY! In my opinion, the acceptance of the human nature is the reason we say we "Can't." Or it is the reason we say it as frequent as we do. Try to follow me!

"I cannot do this because…"

"I cannot forgive her because…"

"I cannot build it because…"

I blame the "I can't" phrase on the knowledge of the human nature. It is my belief that these restrictions within the "human nature" have caused us to naturally doubt our abilities to have control in circumstances separate from activities we cannot obviously perform naturally. What we focus on expands, right?

It is a very important point. I will say it in another way in case you missed that.

I understand that I may not be able to fly under my will alone, but the history of doubting this or the history of doubting anything obvious could potentially increase my overall doubt, affecting every area in my life with unreasonable doubt.

In addition, the snowball effect, which would be applied to "having knowledge of doubt" can have an impact in other circumstances. Could this be the development of the "I can't" phrase over time?

The thought would sound like this subconsciously, "Because doubt exists, maybe it applies in this circumstance that is separate from 'flying under my own will'." I choose to apply "DOUBT" in this circumstance. For whatever reason, I made up in my mind in order to justify my actions or the lack of action in this space and time.

I can write this off too. Ooo, I can write that off as well. Don't doubt everything. Question everything, but find the confidence in your discovery to believe what you find to be true at the moment.

Mission:

Find every reason to contradict doubt so you do NOT fall victim to unnecessary doubt.

Take notice to the "I can't" phrase today. Have you ever wanted to quit or change a nasty or bad habit? Did you have a hard time quitting or changing the habit? Of course, because the majority of us lack the confidence to mentally overcome small things. I believe some cases of this are a symptom of the human nature and the restrictions that come with the classification. You can believe that or not. If it wasn't true, why is it a motivational speech can change someone's life? The doubt was removed; the mental block was destroyed either temporarily or permanently. They had what it took to overcome their flaw in the first place. They had no idea until they did.

Remember, I stated something in the nature of, "Successful people usually have an extreme amount of confidence and self-awareness that gives them everything they need to attempt things they normally wouldn't." This idea tends to evolve into something more powerful-- maybe forced appreciation of positive thoughts.

What happens if you contradict some of the concepts you live by? If you free yourself from some standards, it will give you the capacity

The Life That Brightens the Light

to discover your true potential. No limiting beliefs and unreasonable doubts. What if you were to remove or eliminate as much doubt as possible. How far would you go?

My first hour of pilot training in Kissimmee, Florida.

Outside on the pad with the training helicopter filming an advertisement to cover training cost.

When I left high school, and I could no longer join the military, my idea of becoming a pilot was destroyed. I just knew I was never going to fly. Now, it is clear that this was obviously "Unreasonable Doubt."

Let me say that again:

"I JUST KNEW I WAS NEVER GOING TO FLY."

That's a limiting belief and unreasonable doubt. Remember, the example of people having confidence in their odds to win the lottery? If they believe they can possibly win they play, and if they have extreme doubt they do not invest or take the risk. This is the same thing. Remove the unreasonable doubt to at least have the confidence to discover the possibilities. You will NEVER discover your true potential until you discover your true potential.

This extreme doubt controlled my actions of discovering what WAS possible. I didn't search for solutions to the problem. The problem was I didn't have a clear plan to obtain a pilot license because my primary option was no longer realistic and unobtainable in my mind's eye. There are things you CAN do, but you won't attempt them because of the current standards you live according to.

When the doubt was removed, my reality changed. My confidence surrounding the idea changed, and it was much more positive. With that said, not only did I discover piloting was still an option, but this removal of the doubt actually increased my retention of the piloting material I needed to learn in order to become a pilot. I researched the aviation industry and learned I could become a general aviator. A military pilot wasn't the only option. I wasn't totally familiar with the industry, but in my mind, I had already determined I was rejected. Thus, no action was taken. What potential could you be blocking with your current mentality? Changing your mind can absolutely change your reality.

With that said, maybe your life is a game. You versus you!

Remember, the two-bedroom house? We would've never discovered the potential if we never contradicted the existence of the second room. We excused the idea of the house being complete or enough. The only way to discover potential is to discover potential. In the case of the room, if the potential didn't already exist, we found it, but we were able to remove any doubt that the room had more potential. We just needed to see if it could be discovered.

Let's say before we reconstructed the floor plan someone stated, "This house cannot be more than what it already is." They were wrong according to this example because we disobeyed the restrictions and brought value after contradicting what we saw.

So, what is the point with these titles? Where do we go from here?

This is a healthier way of thinking moving forward:

"I am an individual, meaning I am distinct from a group, class, and family. I define myself and I am who I say I am. I am the builder of my reality and me and everything is possible if I believe it. Period."

This idea will cause the opposite. Instead of possessing more doubt there will be less doubt and more confidence. Doubt can take a little seat. If we had to measure the difference of your confidence before and after this new thought process, anything is better than no difference in the measurement of your newfound confidence. Would you agree?

When you discover your true potential, you will have discovered harmony. You cannot discover the new potential until it is discovered. That is the beauty of the *Extreme Power* concept because not only will you be aware it is possible to reveal more but you'll feel much more confident when you have defined who you are, but why? Well, you chose whom you are deciding to be and it didn't just happen. You happened, and with that intention, your life happens exactly the way you envision it.

Life has a real meaning not to mention the excitement in the pursuit of obtaining more from life. You will find happiness in just having a true direction. You'll have a true purpose or you'll have fun seeking it. This is peace and harmony. It is my opinion, that if we would've never subconsciously limited ourselves to humans, we would be more confident as a race of individuals. I think we possess an untapped power with the use of our mind and our current society has diluted the potency of our mental capabilities. This untapped power is what I call

"The Extreme Power."

I don't think we would have incorporated as much negative self-talk or created additional restrictions for our mental abilities, if any. We could be containing something great inside this power we haven't gotten access to yet. A mind is a terrible thing to waste. Hopefully, this is clear, so get inside yourself and change the seeds in the soil as I did for myself.

As humans, why can we not believe in something without a reason to believe it? Why can we not believe in something that we cannot understand? Do we really need to understand it in order to believe it? What if that is one of the key principles that keeps us from assessing this untapped mental power? You wouldn't believe in God without a reason, but you would disbelieve for a lot of reasons until you contradict them. Isn't that something to think about? I believe this is what separates us from the untapped Extreme Power we could be taking advantage of.

What if when we were constructed, we were given the authority to create anything we thought or contemplated? What if this is the Extreme Power? I believe our doubt is a mental virus to our mental power and ability to manipulate reality. That is my Extreme Power concept.

What if belief wasn't a thought and never existed? What if doubt didn't exist (never a thought)? What if we thought and acted as the creator of our reality? What if it was tangible as soon as we thought it and we expected it in reality? But doesn't that sound like the Law of Attraction?

Look around you! Nearly everything we see today in

reality that is manmade started as a thought. Did you ever consider not believing in what you are contemplating could be the resistance against our untapped mental power and our ability to manipulate reality? We do not need a REASON to believe and we do not need to UNDERSTAND in order to believe because we are the authors of the thought. What if we simply believed in ourselves despite what reality shows us? That's extremely powerful information, wouldn't you agree?

Would we tap into the Extreme Power? Could we create the things we truly desire? Would the things we create make us appear powerful to those who follow and respect us as individuals? Would we be placed in a position to change things in a positive way?

When you want a new life, you must NOT focus on your external actions. You don't focus on doing something different in the "OUT" in the world. You must go inside yourself and change you. You created the outcome. You can also change it. You have that authority. This is the law of polarity, but more on than later.

A pecan tree seed will bare pecans when it's time to harvest. You CANNOT cut the pecans off the tree and wish for a change in what the tree will bear. You must change the seeds. Only then will the tree bear a different harvest.

Change the seeds in your mind. These thoughts are affecting your decisions, actions, beliefs, your reality, and your ability to create something with huge potential. Get control over your reality. How? It's as simple as shifting the focus on you. Look into the mirror. Who am I? Who do I want to be? What do I really want? Where do I want to go? What does it take to get there? Have no doubts! Be the change you want to see in the world. Change the seeds. Then receive a new harvest.

It has ALWAYS been about you. Perfect you and you will see changes. Walk in the spirit of self. Get to know yourself. You cannot live with no one until you learn to live with yourself. How can you love someone without loving yourself? Self-care is an expression of self-love. Do you love yourself? Do you know how?

You are in control, so free yourself from negative self-talk and the "I can't" mentality. You have a new understanding. You should be held at your highest potential and seeking it. You should never find yourself shielded from your highest potential. The human nature we understand subconsciously creates a weak mindset. You should feel invincible! You deserve the best. You are special. You are meant to be different. You are unique. You are powerful. You are meant to bring something to the world. You are never stuck. The world needs what you bring. What you bring will give you the life you deserve while helping others, not hurting others or bringing them down. The term "human nature" should be used for communication purposes only.

You should think beyond the natural circumstances and the human nature we were accustoming to. Be invincible. We must feel the strength we possess and believe in it without a real reason and without needing to understand it. This book will guide you to mental freedom while placing you in a position to exercise your mental strength in order to gain and keep control over your reality. It worked for me, and it has given me the life I desired. When you begin to make these changes, old habits will change. Your circle might change. Your appearance might change. Your neighborhood might change. Your location might change. Your bank account should change. However, you will become more harmonious with you and what you deserve. You will begin to attract the right things and the right people to build your deepest desires. They are waiting on you. Are you ready? Are you getting ready? Do you want it? Do you believe this?

I tell people all the time, "Bad things are always happening in the world while at the same time, good things are happening, and they won't be turned off in this lifetime. However, for those attracting positive things, you won't experience the bad stuff very often. Even when things are bad, you can find the good and it won't feel bad at all. Create a healthy environment with all of you."

Remember--never allow your current circumstances to keep you from controlling your future. Never allow your reality to control your thinking because your reality is the proof of what you think. I must repeat that.

NEVER ALLOW YOUR REALITY TO CONTROL YOUR THINKING BECAUSE YOUR REALITY IS PROOF OF WHAT YOU THINK.

Be a creator of reality and not a reactor to reality.

Slowly you will begin shifting from default standards into your own standards. Begin the process now! You are in control. Do you want the control? Have you always had control, and you've created everything you currently have good or bad? Will it change? Have you been the creator the entire time living by your own standards, but these concepts put things into perspective for you? Can you look back and see why certain things in your life have happened? Can you connect the dots? Was it you? Can you release the pride and blame yourself for the unfavorable circumstances you endured? Can you forgive yourself? Will you? These questions could be tough, but they can also free you from mental bondage. The point is, "You, you, you, you, you!" If you are not in control who or what is? You must be accountable.

In the next chapter, we are going to talk more about you.

Chapter 5

Knowledge of Self

"What Is the Power in Self-Awareness?"

What is the power in self-awareness?

Step 1 – You have the power and authority to redefine yourself. Hopefully, the previous chapter cleared that up a bit.

Be who do you intend to be, and don't leave this up to chance. Scrape every single name, title, and label ever assigned to you directly or indirectly. You don't need it. And if you do accept it, question it first. Is it helpful or harmful to you in the acceptance of this title because you are aware that words, titles, and names are only for communication purposes? Can you limit the destruction these titles can have? Or should you simply rescind them all together?

I asked a young lady, "Who are you?" She replied, "Jessica!" I said, "Jessica is your name, but who is Jessica?" She quickly said, "Me." I asked, "Who is me?" She said, "Jessica." I said, "Let me find Jessica on Facebook." I searched for a random Jessica. Obviously, it wasn't her. While showing her my results I asked, "Is this you?" She said, "That Jessica isn't even the same race." I replied, "You told me who YOU are. Here is a representation of who you said you are."

The point is your name isn't who you are. Your family isn't you! It is used to identity you to a certain extent in society. Your name is NOT who you are. If your name does define you and someone else have that name which means you still do not know who you are. Think about that! You didn't name yourself. What does your name mean? Is it a sign of strength or weakness, power or servant? What does it stand for? Your identity depends on it! Or does it? Do not leave your identity up for chance. Take ownership of YOU! If it's just a name have you made that clear? Treat the business of "YOU" just like a business. Put thought in ever part of you. Why?

You get to decide. There is power in this because you are creating the real you. When you buy a car or product it comes with terms and conditions (warranty), right? In this case, you need to know what all the fine print says about you. Who are you? What do you stand for? What do you believe? Can you identify the areas of your life where you were manipulated? What do you really like? What do you really question about life and your existence or your tradition? Don't subscribe without a full understanding of what you are supporting because this is determining who you are. Be the boss of who you are becoming at all times. It's your life. It's your existence. It's your time and it's very limited. That's out of your control, but who you decide to be is NOT out of your control. Take the wheel.

Think of the doctor. Is the doctor a doctor by accident or was it intentional? That doctor went through years of schooling. I am sure it took a lot of concentration to stay consistent; therefore, it is nearly impossible for the doctor to become a doctor by accident. You can be nearly anything you decide to be with enough time and the right information. Even when it comes to your religion, you had to accept it. The decision was presented before you became a true follower. Do you see the power of a decision? You have that power. This is an aspect of knowing who you are. You are becoming aware of the tools that directly impact your life. This is why you have what you have or the lack thereof.

You making a decision is a POWERFUL THING in and of itself. It is estimated that we make 35,000 conscious decisions a day. Let's take an individual that is 30 years old and consider the estimated number of conscious decisions made in just 10 years between the ages of 20 to 30 years old.

In just 10 years, this person has made 127,750,000 conscious decisions. These decisions determine his lifestyle, relationships, health, wealth, and stability in society along with many other things. Imagine what one bad decision can do. How many people are dead, in the hospital, or in prison from one bad decision? With that said, exposing yourself to good or healthy information can make a difference in your life because it will affect your decisions. The next 10 years of life will consist of more than 120-million decisions. Control the overall health of your decisions. I'm assuming you'll make healthier decisions and in turn produce different results. Like changing the seeds planted in the soil. Planting different seeds will yield different results. With that alone this book has exposed enough to seriously impact your life. I can literally stop there, but let's keep going. Krislyn gave me personal financial advice to help my personal financial experience. How could I take this advice in a negative manner if my limited knowledge is shielding me from healthier decisions? Good information will yield a better harvest.

You have power. You are powerful. Your decisions can help or hurt you. They can affect others as well. Imagine the homeless person who now owns a homeless shelter. His bad decisions could have caused him to experience homelessness. That experience forced him to decide on creating shelter for those without shelter. You have the power in polarity. You can make your mess your message. It's NOT over for you.

A homeless mother has shelter and a program to help her because of his decision. Her relief from the outside elements is due to his decision. You have the power to take control of your own life. You have the power and authority to live the best possible life. You can decide because you are powerful. You are NOT worthless. You just need to find your purpose. The answer is within. I am here to help you discover who you are, but you have the answers. Figure it out.

Let's switch gears a little. What about other titles?

Think of what it takes to remove the idea of being a human. It is only a decision. You don't have to announce it or discuss it with anyone. We are dealing with the subconscious mind. I don't know how it works in the background, but I am taking advantage of the benefits. Remember, you don't have to fully understand in order for it to be used to your benefit. However, it can definitely work against you if you are NOT in control.

The Life That Brightens the Light

What do I mean? We place limits on ourselves. We can also remove those limits. You have the power to decide who and what you are. Every day you are awake you make thousands of decisions. Your exposure and influences alter your decisions. Television commercials condition a person's mind just like movies, music, friends, family, and our environment. Do you protect yourself from the effects these devices have on your subconscious mind? You make decisions with your life from your mind which is the soil. Are you aware of every seed planted and watered daily in the soil of your mind? They can grow. Who is the gardener? Who controls the garden? Weeds exist. Insects exist. Someone has to manage the garden. What if it doesn't rain on your seeds? What if the weeds are overgrown?

Your life, in reality, is surrounded by the existence of your decisions and those around you. You are where you are in life because of you, your influences, and your decisions. This book doesn't exist because I didn't apply myself. This book you are reading exists because my intention was intentional. There are influences you know that exist and some that you don't know exist or both. Now that you know this, you must protect what goes into your eyes and ears. It has the ability to condition your mind and alter your subconscious mind. You can condition your own mind. You can decide what is best for you. People cannot defend themselves against threats they don't know exist. You may be new to this type of content. You are NOW aware. What will you do with yourself? You are aware that anything is possible for you. You can have what you please with enough time.

Have you ever been traveling down the road and thought, "Man, I want a McFlurry!" (I get it. Everyone doesn't eat McDonald's, but just follow along.)

Well, you watched the McDonald's commercial last night. Well, you weren't watching television. You were asleep, but your ears still work while you sleep. You aren't dead--just sleeping. Your subconscious mind heard the suggestion and took note of the suggestion.

Then, you played a YouTube video the next morning on your way to work. The 10-second commercial was McDonald's again. You don't remember because that information wasn't relevant to your current circumstance so your subconscious didn't recall this commercial. In fact, you don't even know that happened. Your subconscious picked up someone at work playing his or her music and an ad played. You don't notice the music or the ad, but it's McDonald's again. Your subconscious mind is so powerful.

Your subconscious mind has determined you want this due to the consistency of the information you are exposed too. So, your subconscious accepts this new seed and gives your body the desire. You recognize the desire and say, "Oh, my! I have been craving a McFlurry from McDonald's all week." That's conditioning through marketing and advertisements. Your subconscious mind has finally accepted the suggestion. Your subconscious mind controls your emotions. When the thought was accepted it gives your body the feelings you feel and consciously you justify them incorrectly. Incorrectly? Yes, because you didn't know you were being programmed to think along these lines. However, you did recognize that you were craving a McFlurry. You decided to justify this emotion with, "I have been thinking about this for a while now." You haven't. You just used this conscious thought to justify and support your emotions.

And back to the point. You get to decide.

The power of a decision along with the law of polarity and the knowledge of having the ability to redefine who you are is a great start to a new beginning. You can begin to identify yourself. You can begin to protect your subconscious mind as well. If you don't like the life you have, you have the power to change that. You may be able to look back and determine how you ended up where you are in life with this new awareness.

I have mentioned this before, but one of the natural laws in this life we live is called "The Law of Polarity." The law of polarity says that everything has to be dual. Everything has an opposite. How can you be inside without an outside? How can you go up unless down exist? If heat doesn't exist, how does the cold? Just as dark can't exist where light does. The negative and positive is the same thing, but are indeed opposites. So, if you don't like your circumstances choose the opposite of your current results. You are never stuck.

I'll say that again:

"YOU ARE NEVER STUCK."

You can choose. There is power in a decision. You are powerful. If don't like being cold, make your environment warm. If you hate being broke, you can become wealthy. Polarity. You can choose. So again, you are never stuck. Choose the opposite. Polarity is a law.

The economy is crashing while someone else is scraping in gains. Polarity. The economy crashing could be scary to you, but in order for a new economy to emerge, we need the old one gone. There are people whose lives are crashing, but it propels them in a new direction. There have been many cases where the new direction saves their lives. Remember, most people don't actually change until hitting rock bottom. Look at Covid-19. How many people took a course or changed careers? Are you seriously ready for change? The time is now.

(Extreme negative and extreme positive.)

Why do you suppose people usually hit rock bottom before making aggressive changes in their life? Do you think the law of polarity had something to do with that? Their circumstances are no longer allowed to continue a path on the extreme negative, so what is the opposite of extremely negative? That's powerful, right? If the extreme negative didn't kill them, they will see the opposite. What doesn't kill you makes you stronger, right? In my opinion, it is according to the law.

Make a decision. Redefine who you are. Scrutinize the person you are intending to be and why. Change your settings. Change the seeds in the soil. You may possibly need new people in your life. Switch things up and DO NOT BE AFRAID OF CHANGE. It is definitely uncomfortable, but this is where we grow and develop. Be comfortable being uncomfortable. You cannot experience serious growth in your comfort zone. It's impossible. Are you comfortable where you are in your life right now?

Step 2 - What do you like? Who are you? Who do you want to be?

Now that you are not tied down to names, titles, and labels, who are you? How do you see and define yourself? When people ask me who I am, I respond, "I am whomever I decide to be." Then, they say, "And who's that?" I say, "Whatever I decide to be at that time."

You must look deep within yourself and ask, "Who do I want to become?" How do I want to be remembered? Spend time with yourself alone. Go through your thoughts and memories. You have everything you need inside. You need to dig even if you need counseling because everyone should seek counseling or a therapy session at least once or twice a year. This is a very healthy idea to consider. Society has given therapy and counseling a negative connotation that something is wrong with a person who requires therapy. In reality, we all could use counseling--even completely healthy individuals. What's under the hood? This is information consumed by our minds as they are manipulating our reality. Trauma is real. How do we let go? How do we discover what is planted deep inside the mind sabotaging our reality? You need to know what's under the hood. Counseling or therapy could reveal the framework that is making your existence haunting.

If you wish to seek counseling the person I would recommend is Latoya Oates. You can find her at www.NewRulezAcademy.com...

Let me show you something about yourself. You may or may not have noticed this about you. I want to show you the real you. You must know whom and what you are deep down inside. This is going to be a powerful tool.

The Life That Brightens the Light

This is an exercise.

I want you to verbally say, "*POWERFUL.*" But when you say it, don't use your mouth. Do not use your vocals/voice. Count to 3 and then say it loud inside yourself (say it in your head). Here we go!

1, 2, 3… P-O-W-E-R-F-U-L

So, did you hear yourself? Do it, again…

1, 2, 3… P-O-W-E-R-F-U-L

You probably said, *1, 2, 3* as well, in your head.

The Voice

Did you hear yourself in your head? You just spoke without using your voice when you said, "*POWERFUL.*" You are reading my book right now. Are you hearing yourself say the words inside yourself? Can anyone else hear you reading this or are you reading this in your head? Listen to that voice. You DID NOT USE YOUR VOCAL CORDS. You have the power to speak without using the physical body. Who is that? What is that? Who do you sound like? The voice you heard is the REAL you underneath the flesh. The flesh is just a vehicle used to be a part of this realm. It's NOT you. It's your vehicle to move about the earth. The body holds your spirit in this realm. When you leave the body your spirit is released and you cannot be held captive to this realm without this vehicle.

The Ear

Now, since you heard yourself say "*POWERFUL,*" you can actually hear without the physical ear. You spoke without the tongue and you heard it without the vibration on your eardrum. Who is that? That is the real you. The body is an extension of who you really are. You are NOT your body. It's a suit. It comes from the earth and it will return. So, with this said, "Who are you?" The body is the limited version of you in this dimension. The real you (*P-O-W-E-R-F-U-L*) aren't as limited as the flesh, but we allow ourselves to be. We think we ARE our bodies.

This isn't so… You can hear and speak without the body. That's a powerful thing.

When *P-O-W-E-R-F-U-L* (YOU) speaks *P-O-W-E-R-F-U-L* (YOU) make things move. The bible says, *"We have the power of life and death in the tongue."* Were you ever speaking on the topic of a person, place, or thing and it came up? You spoke something into existence. This is your strength. It's a tool. A magic wand.

Example:

While sitting in the mall and discussing my co-worker named "Josh" when he actually walked out of the food court several minutes later. P-O-W-E-R-F-U-L. I spoke Josh into existence. You have that authority. You can believe it or not. Use it to your advantage. This book will make you aware of your power and authority.

When you speak, speak from the capacity of *P-O-W-E-R-F-U-L* (THE REAL PART OF YOU). Feel this strength. Feel the power of the real YOU. Use it when you speak. Speak boldly and powerfully.

You have the power in your decisions. You have the Law of Attraction. You have the Law of Polarity. You have control over your subconscious thoughts. Positive self-talk. You have the real YOU (*P-O-W-E-R-F-U-L*). This is the part of you who speaks without the tongue and hears without the ears. The REAL you! You are NOT your body. The body is limited. You are NO longer limited in your mind, body, or your spirit. You are seriously powerful. You are NOT human. The human is the vehicle. It's NOT you.

Who do you want to be?

* The Law of Polarity
* The Power of Decisions
* Self-Awareness

The Life That Brightens the Light

* The Withdrawal of Titles
* Protecting Your Subconscious Mind from Conditioning
* And You Have Discovered Something About Yourself (P-O-W-E-R-F-U-L)

You have a clean slate. We have covered the internal side of the new success you are about to create. You should always change the seed to change the results. Let's work on the physical applications.

Who do you wish to become? What is success?

Success is defined as the accomplishment of an aim or purpose. Where does the aim or purpose come from? Who determines that? Obviously, the answer is "You!" Would you have known that before getting through the contents in this book? This book is about, you, you, and you.

Let's help you determine what success is:

These are the physical corrections you must understand and control. The next step is to help you to redirect your time and actions according to the things that really matter to you. How are we going to do this?

Priorities – Goals – Plans – Daily Agenda

These are sheets you will create and structure. This is the action part of the book. Now that doubt is removed and you know who you are, let's use this advantage to acquire a new life. You are going to follow these steps. They will make a huge impact on your current reality. Even if you DO NOT follow the steps continue to read the rest of the book. You'll get an understanding from this content. When you are ready and willing; you know where to come to contrive a real plan that's packed with purpose.

Priorities are the things that matter more than anything in the world. You cannot die without accomplishing this--*priority*. You may require a personal and a business priorities sheet depending on how much you want to accomplish. Brainstorm both, but build out one sheet at a time to get the process. If your priorities and goals don't scare you, they are NOT big enough. You are powerful, and you can do and be anything in this world.

The first step in the development of your priorities sheet is to spend a few days jotting down everything you want and need to accomplish. "Everything" literally means EVERYTHING you want to accomplish. You must spend a few days brainstorming. It doesn't matter how big or small this task is--write it down! You will think of things tomorrow that you didn't list today. Give it time. Be patient with yourself.

The second step is to create a goals sheet. What do you want to accomplish? These goals will be based on what you listed as your top three priorities on your priorities sheet. This is the desired result on a short-term, mid-term, and long-term timeframe.

When you create the goals sheet, it needs to highlight the things that matter to you in the pursuit of your priorities. As one of my top three priorities I might have that I want to accumulate a following of one million individuals. So, the goal would be to hit the first tier, which could be to accumulate the first 10,000 followers. It highlights what matters to me because one million is excessive, but it is my priority. You eat an elephant one bit at a time and not in one sitting. So I would be going in the right direction if I can hit my first tier in six months to a year. We are definitely going to dig into goals with great detail.

The third step is to contrive the plans in order to accomplish any of this. If you fail to plan, you are planning to fail. So, if you are an individual reading through this book without following these steps (unless you already have a plan) you will see how NOT having a tabulated plan can and will hurt your mission. In the construction of this sheet, it will require weeks, months, and possibly years of research because this process never ends. The more detailed this plan is, all the clearer your direction and vision will be. You can also expose the risk and create a process to avoid or withstand the potential pitfalls. This is a huge advantage of having a tabulated strategic plan. Also, you will have a step-by-step system to follow once the research phase is complete. There are too many benefits of a rock-solid plan for me to list here.

The fourth step to the process that this book will expose is the daily agenda. Now, you have your top three priorities. You have your mini goals, which is a fraction of your ultimate goal (your priority). You have a highly detailed plan on how you intend to accomplish these tasks. Next, we need to take more action. We must create a daily agenda.The daily agenda is a calendar/sheet and, on this calendar, you'll have all the activities and the tasks that MUST take priority over your day. Every day you must have a task on your daily agenda that pertains to your Priority Sheet, Goal Sheet, and Plans. This approach assures that you use every day to build what matters the most to you. This approach makes it nearly impossible to *not* accomplish your goals. How? Well, because you are actively building what you want, and you are being specific as to what you wish to create.

That is the entire process. The only thing you can do from here is to keep your sheets up-to-date and evaluate your plans as things change. You should spend time with these sheets daily or at least every other day. Put in the work to get your sheets as detailed and accurate as possible. Remember, these are the methods I deployed to get the life I have today. I wasn't reckless. My plan and the steps I took were strategic and calculated. Therefore, when someone on the outside looking in had a lot of doubts about my choices I was confident they doubted my choices because they didn't know the plan of attack. My life didn't just happen. I created it. You can too. Let's keep going...

I have a question. What is your biggest asset? Most people give the wrong answer to this question. Is your biggest asset your house? Think about it. You are not renting. You are building equity, right? Is it your car? Maybe you are not paying payments and you own it free and clear. Your transportation costs are super low because of this fact. Maybe your biggest asset is your 401k or your ROTH IRA account. It must feel good knowing you are securing your future. What is your biggest asset? Is it an apartment complex you own? This can be a tax shelter along with the monthly income it produces for you and your family giving you financial freedom and time freedom.

It doesn't matter what you think your biggest assets are. If you didn't say "Time" was your biggest asset, you are about to learn a very important lesson. This tip is everything. There is no asset GREATER than your time. I MUST repeat that:

"THERE IS NO ASSET GREATER THAN YOUR TIME."

Money can be shared, replaced, borrowed, lent, lost, rented, bought, or found. You cannot borrow time. You cannot share time. You can NEVER get back the time you lost. When the clock stops, the game is over for this lifetime. Why would anyone say, "I'm killing time?" Nope. Time is killing you. LITERALLY!

Therefore, your time is your greatest asset. I made a mistake once. My superior once told me it would be easier for her administrator to get her groceries delivered. Without much thought I disagreed because I knew how close the store was to her home. Then, it was broken down.

Let's say you stop what you are doing around the house at 6:00 p.m. You take about ten minutes to get prepared to get outside the house and into the car. 6:11 p.m., you start the car and begin the drive. You are out the car and walking to the door of the establishment nine minutes later. 6:20 p.m., you enter the store and it is Tuesday and somewhat busy. It takes you 30-minutes to arrive at to checkout with your cart semi-full. 6:50 p.m. you are in the line waiting to be checked out. You are loading the groceries into the car at 7:03 p.m., and you are starting the car to leave the property at 7:06 p.m. Then, you pull up to the house and cut the engine at 7:16 p.m., and at 7:31 p.m. you are done putting the groceries away.

That was 1 hour and 31 minutes of your time and if you were to do this twice a week that is three hours of your time. That would equal 12 hours a month. 144 hours in a year or 6 days you missed with your kids, studying, working, or whatever is on your priority sheet.

The Life That Brightens the Light

When you get your list delivered, it takes 5-10 minutes to order and 5-7 minutes to put away. That equals 17 minutes of your time and if you did this twice a week that is 34 minutes of your time. 2 hours and 16 minutes a month or 1 day and 3 hours in a year you missed doing the thing that matters the most.

Six days in a year you missed or one day and three hours. That's the comparison.

When you are a busy person, every second should matter, right? This is a great way of respecting your time. Do you truly understand the value life holds if you waste a second of your time?

Do you truly value your life and your time? Every little bit of effort is evidence that you care about your life and time. If you know exactly what your priorities are, you can maximize your time and do more of what matters and less of what doesn't. Your children could be a priority or your family. This system helps to identify what matters most and the daily agenda helps you to take more action on those priorities. Maximize your time and effort. You may want to consider a personal and a business version of this system. Trust me. If you are NOT managing your time you have lost a portion of your greatest asset.

My question to you is this: "Do you really value your time and your life?" Time management and planning say's that you care about your life. You don't have to tell me. Your actions speaks much louder. Planning is bigger than an organization tactic. In addition, learn to value others time.

Let's go to the next chapter to dig deeper into this system.

Chapter 6

Strategy

"Priorities"

The priorities section of this book is a very important aspect of your future because this will determine where the majority of your time and energy will be spent. I think it is safe to say that if you have enough time, there isn't much you cannot accomplish. As an example, let's just say, "We will all live for 1,000 years." If this was true, one could decide to become a pilot the first 100 years of his life, a doctor for a period of 100 years, and a lawyer for another 100 years. The point is that with enough time you can do and become anything. The issue you are faced with today is that our time, which is our greatest asset, is very limited. Our time is so limited, and we don't even know how much time we actually have. If this reason is NOT a good enough example of why you must manage your time wisely then what is?

Do you recall when I mentioned that what you need is on the inside of you, and I'd use my system to bring that information to the surface? Well, this is that process. You must have a general idea of what is important to you and what you would like to accomplish more than anything in life. Did you know there are many people in life experiencing some confusion with this process? It's called *"The Clash."* There could be many things you would like to accomplish in this life and time, but the two worlds are clashing. What two worlds you may ask? On one hand, you know exactly what you'd like to be doing and on the other hand there is the reality. What you want isn't impossible; the issue is timing, current circumstance, capital, and convenience, along with many other obstacles that could obstruct you from pursing your true desires. You know your fact pattern better than I do, and you have an idea of what's holding you back (*even if the previous chapters pointed the finger at you*). However, the clashing worlds must end.

This system will help you to navigate your desires and help your choices to become more realistic and clear regardless of where you are in your life today and regardless of the current hurdles you must jump to reach them. First, let me further explain the *"Two worlds clashing"* concept. Using me as an example, this is my two worlds clashing:

I seriously wanted to get my pilot license to fly helicopters, but on the other hand, I didn't even have a valid driver's license and a bunch of other debt. If I had the driver's license, I could take advantage of better opportunities and even see my children more often. However, flying helicopters are my dream, and it's eating me alive not to be in the cockpit.

This is a picture of me with my first pilot log
where I track training hours in flight.

I could put time aside and work on the driver's license, but then I'd be giving up time as a pilot. Time is vital because I am already in my 30's playing with the idea of going to helicopter training. This is the importance of knowing what your priorities are and putting thought into what is more important and why.

My two worlds were clashing. My dreams were calling me and it was very enticing, but the fact remained that it made much more sense to retrieve my driver's license first and then revisit the piloting idea. My driver's license cost over $3,500 at the time. Plus, I needed to purchase a vehicle immediately after. Was I expecting to walk to helicopter training? The worlds are no longer clashing and the choices that were made makes my life easier and my goals are much more attainable.

Priorities help to keep you focused on the things that matter the most saving you from wasting time and valuable resources. Not to mention, it forces you to actually think about your decisions. Trust me I do understand choices can be very tough most definitely when it comes to life decisions. If you do the work, this will become much easier. So, let's get started.

This is currently an exercise because you are about to pull out a piece of paper and tabulate every single thing you want to accomplish. To be honest, it might as well be a notebook.

Which priorities should you write down? It does not matter how big or small the priority is--you must write it down and give it a number. Keep in mind, if you don't write it down on this sheet, you will not spend time on it and no thought goes into it. You may need to separate certain priorities. You may need a personal sheet and a business sheet or whatever additional categories you deem necessary. This is about your wants and needs. Do not forget to number each entry! They are NOT required to be in a specific order, but they do need to be numbered.

You don't want to rush this. Be patient and keep these sheets close to you for about a week or better. Go through your days trying to add to this sheet as often as possible. Put some serious thought into what you want to list as a priority. I shouldn't have to give you examples of what a priority is because everything you need for this system is inside you. This process will bring it all to the surface and you'll scrutinize it. Then you will decide what the best course of action is.

When I created mine, I had so many ideas I had no clue how to organize it all. That's the reason why you must list everything. I don't want you to structure your entire plan and forget things that will cause you to rework your sheets later. You are about to do a lot of work to make your vision crystal clear. You can be confident when you are done with this process that every decision you are making is for a good purpose. You will be clear in that purpose. Have you ever been in a place like this in your life? This is the point where everything is tabulated, contemplated, planned, structured, tracked, and evaluated as you work through the steps to complete the project. This is your life. If you haven't been here before, you are about to experience real focus and concentration. A major benefit to this is you know the end result when you have done the work. The end result of your plans is whatever you planned.

Have you listed everything the big goals and the small ones? Did you need to separate business and personal? Organize your categories as you see fit (for example, school, investments, debt, credit goals, parenting goals, vacation goals, and income goals). Keep in mind that this is the priorities list.

So, I am going to assume you are done tabulating everything. This is going to be the thinking phase. Now, ponder everything you have written down. You must realize you only have one life. You may or may not have enough time to accomplish it all in this lifetime. If you know there are some tasks on this list that you are NOT going to have time for in this lifetime, you must scratch it off forever. This could change in the future. Your focus could be so incredible; you remove all the distractions and become highly successful at one thing and it frees you to do EVERYTHING you ever wanted to do. This is NOT unlikely, but for now, you need to be thoughtful about where your time is invested (NOT TIME SPENT). In my opinion, spending time is losing while investing is gaining something. You should invest your time where it actually matters. This will help you to determine what really matters.

So, you know much better than I do. What is not greater than the most important task on your list? Do you have goals so important you can immediately eliminate several little things? You also need to have a full understanding of the pros and cons of accomplishing certain task or goal. How will accomplishing this set me up for the next task and the task after that?

I must refer back to my pilot license vs. my driver's license. The driver's license gave me immediate basic benefits that I lost with the driving privilege itself. The pilot license wouldn't fill the gaps created by the loss of the driver's license. Why would the pilot license trump the driver's license? It wouldn't. I wouldn't even generate an income with the reception of my pilot license. So, it didn't make sense to pursue the dream YET! On the other hand, I could make more money with the driver's license. This directly affects the pilot's license in a positive way because I needed to raise the capital to train. The school has to be paid. A vehicle will give me a better opportunity to make more money. On the topic of priority, there would be no way to make the pilot license make sense against the driver's license.

This sheet forced me to postpone the idea and helped me to recognize what was more important. This was a temporary circumstance because it wasn't impossible to reinstate my driver's license. However, it did cost time and money. Do you know the pros and cons of each task? Are you setting yourself up for success OR are you hindering yourself?

Ask yourself these questions:

What do you care about the most on this sheet?

Why do you care about this ONE specific task/goal?

What do you get out of this?

What would you be risking or giving up in order to accomplish this?

How bad do you want it?

Is it worth the time it'll take to accomplish it?

Are you willing to take the risk?

Have you weighed the risk against the rewards?

The Life That Brightens the Light

Are you sure this is what you want to pursue?

Think deep! Ask yourself as many questions as you can.

It would be wise to put every task and goal through this kind of scrutiny. You need to know why this is your priority. Have you separated your wants from your needs? In most cases, you cannot simply attack your wants without satisfying your needs (every case is different). I just want you to consider this before moving on. You can live without the things you want, but you need what you need. Can you eliminate the wants? Are you willing to give them up? It is perfectly fine if you have time for everything, but if you do NOT have time for every priority and goal, how will you find the time? Do not stretch your focus and concentration too thin. The point is to properly concentrate your time, energy, effort, and attention. Get rid of the things you don't see as an immediate priority.

I remember a businessman said this, "I don't have time. I am always busy, but I make time for the things I want and need."

This is why it is important to begin the process of being honest with yourself. The honesty you have with yourself is about to change your life because you can focus on what really matters. At this point, more energy is being concentrated to a vital aspect of your life and circumstance. This is invested energy. You are NOT wasting it anymore. You can have complete confidence that what you are working on will make a difference because you know your priorities. I will NOT be surprised if you take a totally different approach to your life. It won't look the same a year from today. Mines sure doesn't. I am actually surprised how far I've come. Let's move on!

At this stage of the process, it is important to place every item in chronological order and in the order of its importance to you. Afterwards, the next phase will narrow this list down. Right now, it is your job to take this list and number them according to their importance to you. You may need to rewrite your list and on a separate sheet place your priorities in the order of its importance to you. If you have several sheets (i.e. Workout Sheet, Personal, Business sheets, etc....) you will need to find a way to consolidate these sheets into one or have two sheets and divide your days into two separate agendas in just one day. The point is to be creative in making these sheets applicable to your life, time and schedule.

#1 is #1 when it comes to your priorities. Nothing matters more in your life than this task. What you place in the #2 spot is the second most important thing in your life and so on. Remember, number one means, NOTHING IN THE WORLD is more important (not one person, place, or thing). Once you completed that, we will begin to narrow this list down to your actual priorities.

I must point this out!

Your priorities should support a new way or a new life. If my #1 priority was to make money while I sleep imagine how much I could do once I accomplish this task. So, the point is make sure the #1 priority sets up the rest of your wants and desires. Get crazy and creative.

I need you to follow this concept as a guide to successfully narrow these priorities down to three to five primary priorities. You should've numbered all the priorities you have on your sheet. If you have 100 priorities pick random numbers. In this example, I pick 50, 30, 25, 15, 10, 5 and 3. These numbers represent the priorities remaining on your sheet.

Example:

If you have 100 priorities listed on your sheet you are going to eliminate 50, leaving 50 priorities remaining on your list. The next number is 30. If you have 50 priorities remaining on your sheet you are going to eliminate 20 more leaving 30 priorities that remains on your list and so on (25, 15, 10, 5, & 3). Every priority listed past 15 isn't important and will be forgotten.

Congratulations! You are left with your top 3-priority list, top 5-priority list, top 10-priority list and your top 15-priority list. Now, you

The Life That Brightens the Light

must classify every Top List.

Example:

Top 3 Priority List is the primary list.

Top 5-Priority List is secondary (*This list consists of your top 3, plus the other 2 priorities*). Top 10-Priority List is just a list...

You have reached a point in your life where you should recognize everything that matters. If it isn't on that list, you have invested enough time in thought to realize why it is not as important to you or at least not anymore or until your current priorities are satisfied.

NOTE:

Your priorities may change over time from time-to-time. This is totally fine as long as you are in control and you have a plan.

It is important to read the next paragraph ONLY AFTER you have completed all the previous steps.

If you haven't done the steps in the previous paragraphs, do not continue. If you are truly ready to change, you will write down the answers to the questions posed here. Be honest with yourself! Don't skip this step. Trust the process.

Write down the questions and answers:

1) Why are these Top 3 Priorities so valuable?

2) What are the benefits to accomplishing these priorities?

3) What are the risk involved with pursuing these priorities?

4) With knowledge of the risk involved why are these priorities still worth it to you?

5) How much time do you think it'll take to accomplish these priorities?

NOTE:

Be honest with yourself. Remember, time is your greatest asset. You are weighing these priorities against your greatest asset.

6) What are the consequences of not accomplishing these priorities?

7) As it pertains to your priorities, is it worth being negligent or irresponsible?

8) Are your priorities realistic?

9) Can you seriously accomplish these priorities? Why or why not?

10) Will you have enough time to accomplish these priorities?

- Did you write down all the questions and all your answers? -

These are the questions you should ask yourself after you have narrowed your list down to 3 – 15 Primary Priorities.

Do not continue reading until you have followed all the steps of the system up to this point.

You have successfully completed the most important task. Once your priorities have survived this line of questioning, you've officially created and identified solid priorities. Nothing in your life is more important than the priorities on this list. I cannot express that enough. Everything will try to take your attention from these priorities, but NOTHING IS MORE IMPORTANT. Let's get focused. Remember, you know exactly what you'll earn when you complete these priorities. You are literally in control of your destiny.

The Life That Brightens the Light

If you have created separate categories, you must complete this process for every category. I can't tell you specifically how to organize your life, but you really want to focus on 3 Primary Priorities or figure out what works for your fact pattern and what doesn't.

NOTE:

Let's say for an example if I have a Top 3 business, Top 3 Personal, and Top 3 College... I'd probably take the first one from each list and focus on that as a primary if it makes sense. I think you are smart enough to figure that out.

Let's head over to the next step!

Chapter 7

Strategy

"Goals and Plan"

GOALS

The next step is to figure out your goals. This can be very tricky because you are the only one who can describe the goals you can create out of your top 3 priorities. You cannot have a goal that is not affiliated with your top 3-priority list. I will give you an idea how to create your goals.

Example:

My #1 priority is to make it into the NBA. Therefore, my short-term goal would be to run 5-miles every day. My mid-term goal could be to apply at my favorite colleges and eventually end up on the basketball team. My long-term goal could be to play above average on the team on a college level.

My priority is the end result in this example. You must have a short-term, mid-term, and a long-term goal for every priority. I want you to take notice, in this example; my goals are small steps towards my desired end result (the priority). You must also use deadlines for all of your goals or your goal is only a dream or a wish (it's not real).

You have a good example of how to create your goals so get started. For those with separate categories, I hope you have figured out how to isolate the top three.

Your top three priorities are to be monitored at least on a weekly basis. Your goals are to be monitored at least every other day because they will change. You may have to make small changes based on your pursuit and what you learn along the way.

I have found that as I go through my week, there have been times, I take a look at my Top 3 Priorities List and somehow, I have gotten off track. If this NEVER happens to you, I will be very impressed. Consistency is very powerful in this process.

I want you to realize that you are more focused and in harmony with your purpose than you have ever been in your life with this system. Even if you have always been on track, you at least have a better understanding of your direction and why. In addition, you'll know what you are giving up if you stop your progress or get distracted. Once you get a little further in this process, you can take aggressive action or moderate action. This only determines the speed in the direction you are traveling. Remember to take as much time as you need to really figure out what goals would benefit you more along with the reason why it would. Do not rush this process.

When you create goals, make sure you picked the best goals for your priorities and circumstance to give you the most leverage.

PLAN

The next step in the system is having a *"Rock Solid"* plan. I am assuming you have your goals all tabulated. Good job! This is a lot of work. Would you agree?

Now, you need a step-by-step plan that's written down to determine how you will go from where you are to the end goal. Let me help paint a picture of how a plan works.

Imagine a Global Positioning System (G.P.S.). In order to determine your start and ending point, you need a starting position and a destination, right? You MUST know or at least have an idea where you are and a final destination. How accurate can a G.P.S. be without these two primary points? This is how important your starting position and final destination is in your strategic plan. Where are you in your life, right now? What disposable resources do you have available or the lack thereof? Will you have the time? How would one calculate this without a plan? I imagine they'd guess if they even stop to take this into consideration.

Once you have a starting and ending point, you need a route to get you the desired result. In this case, you want to arrive at your goals or destination in a safe, but swift manner without risking too much time and resources, right?

Think about that! A G.P.S. gives you options on specific routes based on the current road conditions. It helps you to avoid heavy traffic, dead ends, detours, traffic collisions, and routes that are NOT in the direction of your final destination. It gives you confidence that you are travelling in the right direction even if you are not familiar with your surroundings. Also, it has the ability to give you updates to the current traffic conditions as you travel. That means you might have to take an alternate route, which has slower travel speeds, but it's much faster than the original route due to delays. This is the power of a G.P.S. device.

This is the exact benefit you can expect to enjoy with a "Rock Solid" strategic plan. Look at the power and control you have over your destiny when these advantages are deployed. You need a plan and if you don't have one or if you don't have a rock solid plan you are planning to fail.

Rock solid plan simply means you have conducted the required research to avoid the necessary pitfalls, dead ends, and delays that may exist. So you cannot just have a plan. You MUST do the work required to have a foolproof plan of action.

Yep, "ACTION" is another huge requirement. It's so basic and easily looked over. The basis of having a plan is giving you a set of tasks in a well-thought out chronological order. This is because a G.P.S. is useless if you don't plan to begin traveling in the direction of your final destination. In other words, your plan will incorporate steps you MUST take, but these steps are useless if you don't take one step after another.

I hope the G.P.S. example made the advantages of a *"Rock Solid"* strategic plan clear. Are you ready to take massive action? Again, once you have a plan you can begin taking moderate or aggressive action.

I really want to drive this point; a lot of research will be required. In addition, you MUST evaluate your plan on daily *because things change*. Remember the G.P.S. example? I mentioned how the G.P.S. monitors the current traffic conditions as you travel. That's your job! How are things changing? Are prices going up or down? Are qualifications changing? Are companies shutting down or changing their policies? How are these changes affecting your plan? Is it helping or making things much tougher? Did you pick up some new resources or making more money? These new circumstances can alter your plan a bit. Be prepared for these scenarios. Have a plan B, C, D, and E. Things doesn't always go as planned, and that's totally fine because we are expecting things to go sideways. This is why I love the game of chess. The best chess players can see 10-20 moves ahead. If something changes, they alter their next several moves in an attempt to protect their end goal. Stay ahead of your strategy. When things change that is okay. Make the necessary adjustments and keep it moving.

Also, keep in mind you must get this plan as detailed as possible, and it must be written in chronological order because when you follow these steps there shouldn't be any thinking, guessing, or confusion. That's right! You must do all the research so when you begin taking the steps on your plan, you have already connected the dots. Look at the G.P.S. example. Do you have to question the route the G.P.S. has given you? If so, not very much. This is how your plan should be created. It should remove doubt or question. Of course, you'll evaluate, but that's a totally different task. You are just confirming nothing has changed to affect your end result while maintaining confidence of your position.

The research phase is where you will research and investigate, and *it's okay to be confused temporarily in this phase*. You will take a bunch of information and organize it. The planning portion may sound easy, but believe me it isn't. This step can take a couple of weeks to a few years depending on your goals and priorities. That's right-- a few years. The reason is due to limited knowledge about specific qualifications, resources, information, funds, and everything in between. However, once you have come so far in the process, those elements should become available. Then you'll have the ability to continue planning your strategic approach.

I'll use my story as an example.

Do you know that my plan was originally a 15-year strategy? At the time I published this book I was 12 years into my plan. While in jail, I took the foundation I already had and reconstructed it to my current position. With that said, your plan will take time. If your next question is, "How much time" your plan will give you an estimate.

Don't worry about that too much because the good thing is once you know the first few steps you can begin working the plan as you continue to develop the rest of the steps for your *"Rock Solid"* strategic plan.

A good rule of thumb is to get a rough draft of your plan. You can try brainstorming what needs to happen and the resources you'll need along with the things you already have and/or don't have. Once you have a few steps down, by way of brainstorm, sit down and try to put this in a step-by-step process. Call departments or agents. Send out the emails required and get questions answered. Figure out the addresses you need to visit and write those addresses down or the schedule when classes are available. Duly note when updates will be available and brainstorm ideas and concepts on raising capital you don't have.

I'm going to give you another example to help give you the big idea. Let's use the example of going to the NBA. What were my goals?

* Short-Term – Run 5-miles everyday
* Mid-Term – (Apply) Favorite Colleges; Play on Basketball Team
* Long-Term – Play Above Average (College Level)

The Life That Brightens the Light

Okay, we are going to use these goals as a place to begin our plan. Let's start with running 5-miles a day. What is my current condition (Starting Position)? I eat a lot of junk food on a daily basis, and I do not work out or run. I need to start running and change my current eating habits. A good way to measure my endurance is to run a fast mile. I ran a test mile and I ran the mile in 12-minutes. A healthy man in shape at my age runs a mile in 7-minutes. What I am doing is trying to determine a measurable starting point? Here is how my plan would start out:

* Step 1 – Do research on clean eating and adopt better eating habits
* Step 2 – Start running a mile a day until my time reach 7-minutes
* Step 3 – Do research on shorten my mile run (From 12 to 7-min.)
* Step 4 – Get more sleep - research shows I can run faster times if rested

Those are only the steps for the short-term goals. Let's keep going! Also, notice the comparison of the G.P.S. system. We are finding the starting point and gaining information to determine a route to take based on the final destination.

* Step 5 – What am I looking for in a college? I must start with the B-Ball Team
* Step 6 – Research completed – I need a large school to get noticed.
* Step 7 – Larger schools have more competition

Notice how I am adopting a smarter approach to my strategy as I continue to conduct research? This is the element of the G.P.S. that updates as current traffic conditions change. It will increase the chances of your obtaining and hitting your priority on the money. Also, you'll normally start out with a general idea or goal, and it will evolve into an actual concept or step in your plan of action.

* Step 8 – Find a basketball trainer (fundamental training)
* Step 9 – Can I qualify for a larger school (qualifications increased)
* Step 10 – Find books and resources on finding grants
* Step 11 – Applying at schools and collecting information I'll need

Those are just some of the steps required to get the process started. Did you see how the research I conducted showed that I could increase my chances of getting noticed at a larger school? This new information means that the qualifications are heightened, and I need to determine if I can meet these qualifications. Circumstances can change so easily; therefore, you will be required to evaluate your plan on a daily basis. Discipline will make a difference in your progress as well. Why would I watch television when I could be reading a book on the topic of grants? I could be training with a trainer in order to improve my fundamental skills. There is always something you can do to contribute to your goals and plans.

Remember, this:

"The honesty you have with yourself is about to change your life because you can focus on what really matters. At this point, more energy is being concentrated to a vital aspect of your life and circumstance. This is invested energy. You are NOT wasting it."

It is always best to be honest with yourself. Do you really want this? If I were to spend money on shoes, how wasteful would that be if I could have saved this money for school or for payments for a trainer or books for school or the grant writing process? When your goals are tabulated, it will be easy to identify when you are off task. This is the power of a strategic plan. Just as the G.P.S. warns you when you get off route. A highly detailed plan can provide you a strategic approach to your priorities, and if you were to find yourself off track, the plans make this obvious.

You can control how off task you are. It'll be obvious to you when you are NOT tending to your priorities. It's not just about being off task anymore. You are literally neglecting your priorities. Do you remember this question?

> 7) *As it pertains to your priorities, is it worth being negligent or irresponsible?*

What was your answer to this question? You were asked to tabulate your questions and answers. What do you have? Review it right now!

Guilt will help keep you on track or either you'll say, *"Screw my goals and priorities."* You'll have more accountability. That's the hope!

Let's keep moving through the system.

Your plans will always require research, and at some point, it will require you to learn a new skill. You might even have to change your routine. I told you this book would require you to do tasks that are challenging or outright uncomfortable. In the example, my plans would require me to change the way I eat, begin cardiovascular exercise, and read more books. Not to mention, I would be doing a lot of research. Are you willing to learn something new? The moment you stop learning you have failed. Your strategic plan will keep you accountable. If you are the type that doesn't like learning it's time to change that mindset. Dig into the soil and plant new seeds. You DO NOT know it all. You NEVER will. That means you will ALWAYS be learning. Leave no room for error. NEVER STOP LEARNING!

"THE MOMENT YOU STOP LEARNING YOU HAVE FAILED."

Now, that you are structuring your plans strategically you want to get as far ahead of yourself as you possibly can. What does that mean? If you can structure your plan from beginning to end, do that. When you are done, begin getting the step you are on and the next step as detailed as possible. That's right! Get detailed with your earlier steps! Why?

These are steps you can begin taking now! NIKE slogan is, *"Just Do It."* So, do it! ACTION.

Another approach, depending on how fast you are going through your steps, you can get detailed with the earlier steps and you can be vague with your later steps. However, as you advance through the steps of your plan, those vague steps need to become more detailed. The planning will NEVER stop; remember, I stated you could be planning for weeks, if not years. You must make sure you have the resources you need or figure it out. You must find the capital you need for the things that require it. The point is this--nothing stops the priority from becoming tangible. When you hit a roadblock, you are to structure a plan to get around it. Remember, you are never stuck. Stuck is a mindset. You do not have that.

Let's side track a bit!

Resource: Build winning relationships with people that can help you in areas where you realize you'll need assistance. Don't be afraid to ask for funds you'll need. Never forget that there is no shortage of money in the world. Someone has the money you need and is more than willing to give it to you. Positive energy attracts positive energy. Attract people with the energy you put out into the world. Don't complain and always be positive. This is the Law of Attraction.

There may be a situation where you will need a recommendation. Who can help you? There are people out in this world that were meant to help you. Connect with them. They could be anyone; don't prejudge anyone. Build positive relationships. Also, when these people come along it will be so easy to explain your goals because this system has forced you to tabulate your objectives. Share your goals with those who matter. You will never know what someone can do for you until it is discovered. Put yourself in position.

Let's get back on track!

Why is research important? You will need to know the amounts for fees you'll need to pay. You will need to locate addresses to departments you will need to visit before you actually reach the step. If you need to learn specific laws you need to invest the time to acquire the knowledge. You must go as far as calling to ask questions before you are even close to the steps. You might discover things you will need or information you'll need to know and maybe even qualifications you'll need to meet. Simply put, research gives you a slight advantage. Be sure to position yourself to work on those tasks while working through unaffiliated steps. When you arrive to a new step, there should be no guessing because the work should have been completed already. You just need to follow the steps. Again, things go wrong all the time so you will need to revisit your plan often. It's difficult to stay on track when things go wrong so stay ahead of the curves. Remember the G.P.S.? The G.P.S. consistently monitors the current road conditions to keep you on the safest and fastest route to your destination. In this case, you are the monitoring system that monitors current conditions. Stay on point.

It will get tough at times, but keep the consistency. If it will require more time and there is no way around it, so be it. Keep going! When it gets tough or discouraging pull out the sheet with *the reasons why your priorities are important to you.* Follow motivation speakers online and offline. Get a mentor for your industry because they have the ability to soften the blows you will take. And always stay positive because you have three options.

Why do your priorities matter more than anything in your life? Why is the risk worth it? Remind yourself why you are going through this process. You can allow a small fence to stop you from playing in the park, or you can jump the fence and deal with the consequences later. At the end of the day, what matters more? Hopefully, your priorities.

Again, do all the necessary research and be very detailed. Write EVERYTHING down, or you haven't seriously planned anything. Be sure you have a plan for every step required to accomplish your short, mid, and long-term goals. Find out what could go wrong and get ahead of the issue. Constantly troubleshoot your potential pitfalls and roadblocks. Always play devil's advocate with yourself because it will force you to over prepare which isn't a bad idea. Whatever area you are weak in, you must begin to strengthen. Treat this system like a business and organize well. You are currently the Chief Executive Officer of your life and the priorities of the business life of your life. Be a good leader of your circumstances.

I mentioned, "Whenever you are weak you must strengthened." It puts you in a powerful position when you have the sense to know and understand where your weaknesses exist. Locate them and strengthen them or find a strategic way to compensate for the disadvantage. This will only make you that much more unstoppable. You don't have to know it all. You aren't always required to have the money. People who are willing and able exist. Connect.

You have planned well when you get to the last step and you are a few steps away from your goals and priorities. That's the point! It will mean you have invested a lot of time, but you aren't losing a thing because you considered the risk a long time ago. Reward yourself when you accomplish important milestones. Have knowledge of when these milestones are realized and celebrate *in a way that makes sense to you!* That is very important. Be sure your celebration doesn't take you back steps.

EVALUATE

Next is evaluating. Evaluate. Evaluate. Evaluate. Always evaluate your plan. Things change. Requirements change. Qualifications change. Laws change. Rules change. People change. Time causes things, places, and people to evolve. You thought one thing and it was another. Restructure your plan and make the necessary changes when things go wrong and have options. The idea is NEVER quit and be patient with your plan, yourself, and the process. It will work. So keep working it.

Don't forget you are earning something. Therefore, you are paying for something. The labor is a form of payment for the thing you desire. Have you ever heard the term, "Pay Attention?" Why do you suppose "Pay" & "Attention" has become a common phrase used together? What is paying? Giving value in exchange for something valuable. That's my version of this definition. What is attention? Attention is giving a person, place or a thing your concentrated conscious awareness. This is my definition when you put the two together. Your conscious awareness is so valuable and powerful when concentrated; it is nearly identical to paying with currency. Your attention is powerful. You literally can give life to a thing with your focus and concentration of your awareness. Look at it this way. Thomas Edison didn't give up. He focused on the possibility until it was no longer impossible. If he didn't think about it or if he ignored the idea, we wouldn't enjoy the benefit today. Where would we be without light today? He paid with his attention and we are receiving the benefit.

The point is this; evaluate your plan as often as you can. Giving your plan this time, energy and attention will make a huge difference. It could even shorten the length of time it'd take for your priority to become tangible. It wouldn't hurt to watch YouTube videos, take courses, attention seminars, or read books on planning and time management skills. Increase your ability to produce results. NEVER STOP LEARNING. You will see the benefits of this tip. Trust me!

Let's move on!

Chapter 8

Strategy

"Daily Agenda"

You actually have a rock-solid plan at this stage of the process. How does it feel? Do you feel like you are in control yet? Are you on the right track? I am proud of you. This book gives me a happiness you cannot understand. I want you to win because you are capable.

Are you looking at all the steps but feel like it will take forever to complete it? Do you kind of want to fast-forward? I have been there before. Control those emotions. Don't let them control you. Enjoy the process! Most people think the comfort is going to be at the finish line. Do not be deceived. You are still living. Appreciate all the moments you have right now. Life is still happening around you. Take it in. This process is a part of that life. You must find a way to live while you build.

Life doesn't start when you accomplish your ultimate goal. That is a huge deception. It has already started, so be present for every moment. Find time for family and friends and take reasonable breaks. You can still have a life, but find a healthy balance. Your life is incredible. Keep it that way! Discover yourself and be responsible for the big change of reality. Most people are commonly afraid you'll change when the results are in. Figure out who you are now so when your priorities are tangible, you can be confident the success won't change you in a negative way. Who are you? Why? Because money brings more of whom you are out. This next step of the system is going to keep you accountable and focused on the right thing day after day. So, let's dive in.

Your daily agenda is a planner. Always update your daily agenda the night before in order to plan for the following day. The daily agenda

The Life That Brightens the Light

will consist of tasks that directly address items and actions that must be completed and carried out. These tasks are a part of the plan you created. This would be equivalent to the G.P.S. laying out your route based its finding with the current road conditions.

Your daily agenda addresses other things surrounding your day and not only the task tied to your plans. Think about that. You stop at stop signs and traffic lights on your route, right? You still comply with the rules of the road. Why is this powerful? Your daily agenda doesn't allow you to forget stability task. You got to pay bills, call your service providers, deal with the kids, get the car fixed, go to the doctor, and everything in between, right? Your daily agenda sees to it you do all those things, but you also pencil in time for at least one or two tasks that pertains to your plans. There is ALWAYS a balance. The rule is to never go a day without doing a task that pertains to your priorities, goals, and plans. If you can follow these rules over a long-term, there isn't a reason why you wouldn't accomplish your goals. Stability is something that matters although I don't know your priorities. Find the balance.

So, I will continue to use the previous example we used throughout the book to give you an idea of how the daily agenda will apply:

Let's recap!

    * Short-Term - Run 1-mile everyday

    * Mid-Term – (Apply) Favorite colleges; play on basketball team

    * Long-Term – Play above average

    * Step 1 – Do research on clean eating and adopt better eating habits

    * Step 2 – Start running a mile a day until my time reach 7-minutes

    * Step 3 – Do research on shorten my mile run (From 12 to 7-min.)

* Step 4 – Get more sleep - research shows I can run faster times if rested
* Step 5 – What am I looking for in a college? I must start with the B-Ball team
* Step 6 – Research completed – I need a large school to get noticed
* Step 7 – Larger schools have more competition
* Step 8 – Find a basketball trainer (fundamental training)
* Step 9 – Can I qualify for a larger school (qualifications increased)
* Step 10 – Finding books and resources on finding grants
* Step 11 – Applying at schools and collecting information I'll need

DAILY AGENDA (*The Brainstorm*)

Now it is time to apply these ideas and concepts to our daily lives using a daily agenda. This is another action exercise, which will see that your plan is in progress (ACTION). These tasks directly affect your results. So, let's get to work.

If you recall, my goal in the previous example is to eat healthier. This is perfect because I need healthy carbs for my morning run so my body doesn't feel sluggish. There is a health bar up the street that opened a few days ago. I'll jog there and consume something light. Also, I will try different things until I find something I like. At the same time, I will schedule time tomorrow to learn how to make healthy meals at home to save extra money.

My other goal was to run a mile a day. I ran the mile-run one time in order to time the speed of my mile-run. For the next 7 days, I will pencil in my mile-runs. Before I commit to a specific time, I decide to conduct some extra research. The research shows that running in the morning is much healthier versus running in the evening. That means I can no longer start my day at 10 a.m. I must wake up an hour or two earlier to eat something light and run.

This is going to be a new habit because running is a new priority at this point in my process. My daily agenda will reflect the following: Tomorrow, I will awake up 2-hours earlier than usual and run to the health bar. I will try something on the menu that works in favor of my goals. Tonight I must pick a bedtime that will accommodate this new wake time.

Those are two great examples of the task that starts my agenda every day. If there is a day where I need to travel early in the morning, I can pencil my run at night before bed when I get to my destination. In this example, we can also decide to wake up three hours earlier every morning, but use the extra hour for school research or grant writing time before the morning run. These are some options in order to become more productive. The extra focus on this small task will pay off, but we must invest into the process.

The daily agenda will be a current calendar *either electronic, physical form or both*. I recommend those times and events so you should place them on your calendar and you should follow the program that you've constructed. These are all examples of how to use this system.

Here are some things to think about:
* Plan weekends and holidays (making calls, physical visitations)
* Schedule phone days (office time), errand days (travel required), research only days
* Computer only days (research, applications, emails)
* Priorities, goals, plans, and agenda review day (once a week)

Plan well for weekends and holidays. Don't schedule phone day on the weekends or during holidays because administrative offices and call centers are likely to be closed. Also, be mindful about Mondays after a holiday because most call centers and or administrative offices will be flooded with callers. Be creative with your planning and save time. Schedule to have errands run in the mornings, and the phone calls will be completed in the evenings or vice versa. You could have computer research day on the weekends and visitation to locations in the mornings during the week. Find out what works best for your household and schedule. Also, do not forget to schedule time for review day. Yep, you must take 1 - 3 hours in order to review your priorities, goals, plans, and agenda. There is no telling what you will find. Make the entire process make sense. Walk through the entire plan step-by-step. If things are missing, fix the errors. If steps are missing, create and construct the step in great detail. Keep good notes for yourself when you retire a task. This helps to stay organized and it ensures you don't miss important task or information.

Remember, I stated, "I have found myself off task before?" If I didn't hold myself accountable by scheduling "Review Day," there is no telling how long I'd be off task. I had no idea how I got off task during the week, but it tends to happen. I noticed that phone numbers on the plans changed or operating hours. Evaluate your plans at least once a week (stay on top of your priorities). That is the minimum--once a week. I kid you not--it would take me hours to properly comb through my plans. I would write them down and type them up so I had them in different formats. I took this process very seriously and you should as well. You will begin to wonder how people have a busy life without their priorities, goals, plans, and daily agenda tabulated. Pass them this book! You will make their life much easier.

A person that manages their time well will have a good life. I heard a multi-millionaire once say, "Show me your planner and I'll tell you if you will be successful or not." He could see what you are doing with your time. Obviously, if you have tabulated a strategic plan and you follow it, the outcome is apparent. When you finally know what you are focused on it will be clear to see your future and the direction. Those without this will lose time without knowing they have because they subject themselves to ALL the pitfalls, dead ends, delays, and loss of valuable resources. You can literally spin your wheels (going nowhere) not to mention the direction of travel. You are literally avoiding these avenues. There is power in a strategic plan.

The Life That Brightens the Light

A plan helps you to quickly notice how realistic your goals are, and it should be challenging. Don't be afraid to shoot for the stars or Mars. This simply means aim high. Your priorities should scare you or they are NOT big enough. Think of it this way--if you don't hit mars in your aim, at least you passed all the stars. Use this system to better your life. You are deciding what you want. You are the creator and the author at this point. Most people have visions with no action. You don't only have a vision. You have a plan, and you're taking massive action. That is powerful. Plus, by contriving a plan, this was your first act in action. Now, never quit and keep progressing. This process is why I am currently successful.

I can think back when I first started to promote myself as a singer. Someone asked me, "Hey, I really love your passion for singing. How can I help you on your journey?" I had no idea what I needed or how they could help me. If I did choose something I wouldn't be as confident in their role. I didn't have a plan with a clear vision. Times have changed. I am more prepared than ever before and so are you. Do you remember this phrase: "You are NEVER stuck"? I would much prefer for this to be applicable to my life as I've incorporated a rock solid plan versus living by default (living according to the wrong standards).

Use yourself as an example!

With all the work you have done so far, if I walked up to you right now and said, "Hey, I really love your passion for what you are creating. How can I help you on your journey?" Would you be able to answer that question? Another powerful thing you'd have to take into consideration is you can literally pull out a physical copy of your plans. Not only do you have a plan, but I can see it, touch it, and feel it... You can show me where you are in the process and where you intend to be in the future. You can intelligently explain what you need and why. You can explain to me the risk and the rewards. You can explain where all the resources are and the pitfalls you are avoiding along with a plan (A, B, & C). You can effortlessly explain the changes you've made to your personal lifestyle in order to make your goal more realistic and obtainable.

Did you notice the words I used? You can "Intelligently." You can "Effortlessly." You can "Explain." You know why? This has been a system you've created for your life and you have invested time into this on a yearly, monthly, weekly, or on a daily basis. You know this strategy like the back of your hand and it evolved over time. There are so many benefits to this system. When you explain your priorities to someone willing to listen they will be intrigued. I have been in your position. I speak from first-hand experience.

I want to encourage you to add extra things to your sheets that will benefit you. Eating healthy, reading good books, a life of exercise, a healthy spiritual life, the consumption of motivational content, search for investment vehicles, and even meditation helps. These things cannot hurt. If you really want to be sharp, I strongly suggest becoming a follower of good motivational content. Every day, I watch at least one motivational video. I change up the subject as often as possible. This will make a huge difference in the way you think. Remember, when the mind is conditioned, it affects your decisions. In this case, your decisions will lead you to a healthier lifestyle. There are no limits. The only limits that exist are the ones you create and remove.

Don't forget to challenge yourself. Have you ever thought of writing a book? Do it! What is the worst thing that can happen? You learn from the experience? I'll be the example. I am still shocked I have a published book. I'm not better than you are. You can do this. You can do anything. Do not become relaxed in your comfort zone. You cannot seriously grow in your comfort zone. Don't be afraid to be risky. Attempt things in life that are new and uncomfortable. Be comfortable being uncomfortable. Let's change gears a little bit.

I'll see you in the next chapter.

Chapter 9

Mindset Control

"Conscious & Subconscious Mind"

In this chapter, we only want to focus on the basic operations of the mind. Our brain has a system in place to make operations easy and simple for us as living-beings. The system within our mind is known as, *"The Conscious Mind"* & *"The Subconscious Mind."* This is our main focus.

Disclaimer:

It is strongly suggested that you take this information as something leading you down a rabbit hole. Find resources outside of this book to gain more knowledge on this topic. I will do my best to teach you about the Conscious and Subconscious Mind, but there are stronger resources on this topic. I am only leading you to the water. You know the saying.

The conscious mind is aware of the current moment and you can be aware of most mental functions. When you are not conscious, you are considered to be sleeping, daydreaming, in a state-of-trance, sleep-dreaming, sleep walking, staring off into space, in a daze, or a coma. This is known as, "unconsciousness." If you are not conscious and not in one or more of the states, I listed above, you are dead. Unconsciousness doesn't mean you are not alive because your body functions are functioning. Your subconscious mind takes over until you return to consciousness even if you are awake and not conscious. We will discuss the subconscious taking over a little later.

The conscious mind is the creative mind. This is the part of you that actually thinks. This is the state of mind when you think and make decisions. You are considered to be more mindful in this state. It's simply focusing your awareness on the present moment. When you are thinking, you are *"inside focus."* You may or may not understand what inside focus is, but I have a clever way of explaining inside focus.

At the time I wrote this book I was a student helicopter pilot. As a pilot, while flying through the airspace there is a lot going on inside the cockpit of the aircraft. I have tasks inside and outside the cockpit, but I cannot neglect the activities and circumstances that are continuing to change around the outside of the aircraft. Therefore, we have to concentrate on going back and forth between the cockpit and visually scanning outside the cockpit. When eyes are inside the cockpit, you are watching gauges and temperatures to be sure you are in the aircrafts operating limits and to be sure no cautions are being ignored. Also, we are monitoring the aircrafts' attitude, radios, global positioning system, and radars by looking inside the aircraft. The pilot is temporarily neglecting the circumstances outside the aircraft while the focus is fixed on cockpit functions. If too much time is spent inside the cockpit, it could be dangerous if attention isn't shifted within a reasonable amount of time. Things are changing rapidly all the time. When the pilot is outside focused, they are currently visually scanning which is an important skill used to spot other air traffic and while doing so we observe weather conditions, navigating, listening to our own aircraft and watching out for terrain along with any other obstructions that may or may not exist. As a helicopter pilot, dividing your attention is a skill in and of itself.

So, getting back to inside focus, it's when you are thinking, but you are not conscious and you are not taking in information about what is happening around you. Consciousness is awareness. When you are not aware of your immediate surroundings, maybe you are not conscious of your surroundings while still being conscious. That sounds more like focus, but when you are in autopilot and just looking in the direction of the person talking but you're actively searching your home in your mind for your keys you are inside focused. Just like the helicopter pilot when eyes are inside the cockpit monitoring the gauges, the aircrafts' limitations, and its attitude. The outside circumstances are not being scanned for potential dangers, and navigation efforts are seriously reduced. While you are thinking, the conscious mind, the thinking side of you, is busy and unavailable at the moment. I guess you are wondering how you are operating while you are not available. I mentioned earlier, *"Your subconscious mind takes over until you return to consciousness."*

This is the perfect time to discuss the subconscious mind. This part of the mind is the habitual or the programmed mind; 95% of the things we do is automated and acted out by the subconscious mind. Let me repeat that:

"95% of the things we do is automated and acted out by the subconscious mind."

The key phrase is, *"ACTED OUT BY THE SUBCONSCIOUS MIND."* That means programs that are adopted by your subconscious are acted out by your subconscious and you have very little control *unless you change the programming inside the subconscious.* I hope you caught that. Basically, your subconscious mind have a great idea of who you are at the core and it can determine how you would behave with the given circumstances if you were conscious and the subconscious mind acts that out without your permission.

Side Note:

This is why you must be careful who you spend time with. You can easily become more like them because your subconscious mind records everything. It can even accept behavior from your environment and make their habitual habits your new subconscious program. Ever noticed when you move from one environment to a new one, you pick up on their accent and begin speaking in the new manner you subject yourself too? You didn't consciously decide to speak their slang.

Let's get back on track!

When the conscious mind shuts down or is unavailable, your subconscious mind is who you are so it knows exactly how to honor your standards and morals without your help. You are basically on autopilot when you are consciously thinking while life continues around you. The subconscious part of the mind takes a ton of the workload off the conscious mind because this part of you doesn't think. Our subconscious mind excels when we conduct light, simple task.

The subconscious is accountable for skilled progression, individual growth, and behavioral progress. It's responsible for many habits that you perform and you are unaware of it which I will cover later. Your subconscious is also the memory bank that stores and retrieves your data. What do I mean? In the case of feelings and attitudes, we are designed by our subconscious mind. Your programmed behaviors, attitudes, and emotions stem from the subconscious. Remember, 95% of the time your subconscious is automated and acting out what is inside your subconscious mind.

Let's say you bought a car. The car (*the data*) represents the memory recorded in your subconscious. Let's say, you painted the car red (*processed data*). The paint represents the behavior, attitude, or emotion attached to that car (*recorded memory*). In this case, red is equivalent to hate or anger, and it's attached to a memory of your stepfather. The narrative is your stepfather, and the data and recorded memory and your attitude is the processed data.

So, your mom desperately wants you to accept him or at least act like you like him. The problem is *deep down inside,* your subconscious is responsible for the way you feel, and it's not allowing you to be okay with him. That's the *"deep down inside"* feeling. It vocally sounds like this, "*Mom, deep down inside, I try to be around him and be cool, but when I see his face, I want to _____ him.*"

So, consciously you have agreed to accept him, but the subconscious mind hasn't removed the negative program which isn't in acceptance of your step dad. Your emotions are coming directly from your subconscious, which is telling your body to emotionally feel uncomfortable (anger, frustration, depression, and fear). If you truly want to accept him you MUST address your subconscious programming. Surface decisions won't impact the subconscious mind. Let's go deeper into this topic. When did your subconscious mind begin the initial programming process?

Your subconscious mind began the programming process from the time you were born. Your consciousness wasn't activated until around 7 years old. Your consciousness took your identity from the subconscious programming you received for 7 years of your childhood up until the point where your consciousness was activated. You were getting your programs from your environment, friends, and family before you were 7 years old. Before you turned 7 years old, your consciousness was not activated. It is possible to have accepted programming that is self-sabotaging, flawed, limiting, counterproductive, and much more. Does this sound like a life by default if not addressed?

We touched this topic in an earlier chapter!

This is exactly what I said:

"You can like something because you were conditioned to like it (with or without your knowledge). Is it possible that you have adopted traits, thoughts, concepts, beliefs, habits, or anything that is NOT something you personally scrutinized, accepted, and adopted?"

What was your answer to that question? Is this statement/question more believable now? I sure hope so. All the programming you received wasn't bad. There are also some good programs that stem from your childhood programming during that period. Some examples could be family-oriented, respectful, clean, and honest, along with many other good traits, habits, and behaviors. What positive traits have you taken from your childhood and subconsciously adopted and still live by to this day? This kind of scrutiny is vital to your success because you need to answer the question of who you are. You don't know if you haven't addressed programming that exists within your mind up to this day. Think about this.

I think you understand the inside mind concept, but I am going to drive it home. When you begin to think, at that point, you are consciously inside your mind. Therefore, your subconscious mind kicks in and takes over the outside cockpit actions as your autopilot. Again, the programs in your subconscious lead your life during the time you are thinking. There are several other functions performed by the subconscious mind. I will discuss those later.

Do you think you have to pay a little more attention to the possible programs you've adopted as a child? I hope your answer was a big, "Yes!" When we drive, walk, talk, eat, and watch videos or anything commanding our attention, and we willingly pay, at this time our subconscious mind can perform without our knowledge of it taking place.

Example:

Have you ever driven or walked all the way home, but at some point, you realize you haven't been focused on walking/driving or the conditions of the path you took or the hazards involved? You are sure there were obstacles. You are even sure you went through a few bends and curves in the path, but you didn't really understand how you safely navigated through the course unaware or unconscious. Do not be alarmed because your subconscious had your best interest in mind. Did you know your subconscious has adapted to rescuing you in times such as these? The subconscious mind handles fight or flight responses and all the involuntary actions even while you're conscious.

When you move a body part or limb with a conscious intent, this is the conscious mind. Have you ever been involved in an engaging conversation and limbs continue to move while you speak? This is an involuntary gesture created by your subconscious mind. This is common with people who speak with a lot of body language. You should have a minor understanding of the conscious and subconscious mind. Let's back pedal a little.

Remember, I said, *"You have the power and authority to redefine yourself. Scrap every single name, title, and label ever assigned to you directly or indirectly?"* The focus here is, *"directly or indirectly."* This knowledge of the conscious and subconscious mind gives you awareness of how the programming you received may need to be contradicted or altered. You will always add to your subconscious programming. Who surrounds you? What are the lyrics saying in the music you're listening too? Are your friend's super negative or super positive? These are things to think about among many other things. You can be influenced directly or indirectly. Why do you think students of a given skill locate mentors? They want to take advantage of their ability to adopt good programming from someone who has already mastered the skills they want to acquire. This could be spiritual, mental, emotional, or physical programming. In this case, you are using the advantages of the subconscious ability to adopt healthy habits which are known as mental programs.

What is your mental programming surrounding money? What is your mental makeup of religion? What is your mental programming of family? I could go on and on. Your life is the existence of your decisions you have made over time. You want to be influenced by healthy thoughts, ideas, people, songs, words, affiliations and relationships, but you need to fill your life with this. Pay attention to the tone of your conversations with friends and family. Imagine everything you talk about you would have. Do you want to continue those conversations or change the topic? Watching the news all day and all night influences your reality rather you like it or not (*rather you know it or not*). Watch how people think that read a lot of news. Notice what you'd notice about the things they say and what they believe or the lack thereof. Remember, good and bad exist in the world at the exact same time. Which one would you prefer to visit you and your reality the most? The good or the bad because what you focus on expands. What is going into your eyes and ears? It matters.

You must look at your life like a creator. If you go to school to become a doctor, if you never quit you will eventually become a doctor. If you learn everything there is to know about investing in stocks you will eventually become a multimillionaire trading stocks. All you have to do is invest your time in the knowledge. Some things you'll learn by just being around them. Thank you subconscious mind. How many songs you don't like and you can sing a few lines of it if not the entire song? Focus and create.

Walk in the spirit of you as the creator and author. Always be in the status of building your life and your future. When you don't have money don't mention it. Act like you know you can release money into your reality. Speak it into existence. Speak life into your life. Pay close attention to your self-talk. Do you normally say positive things to yourself and about yourself?

I heard teens say very often, "Oh, my God! I am so dumb. Look what I did." I always explained to him or her the importance of saying positive things to himself/herself and about himself/herself. Random things we say, "He is killing me with that ugly shirt." When you speak like this, you don't have to die, but you could hurt yourself. It could be a repercussion as simple as a minor cut when you speak of *"killing."* You don't have to literally die. However, the repercussion is a measure of the idea. You spoke that into existence. Have you ever been talking about someone, and he called or walked in? Your response was, "I swear I was just talking about you." You spoke him into existence. Everything is connected.

Can you point out anything that is manmade that didn't originally start out as a thought first? You cannot! The tangible thing is usually a result of what the mind contrived. Create something without it being a thought first. In my opinion, this is impossible. I could be overlooking a circumstance where this has happened, but I seriously doubt it. Everything manmade started as a thought. The mind is very powerful and you possess one. A mind is a terrible thing to waste. You've heard that before, right? Does it hit a little differently now?

When bad things are happening, do NOT fix your thoughts, words, or emotions to align with the reality. Stay positive! Keep speaking into existence what you desire and believe it without needing a reason why it will happen how you said it would. Just be confident you'll get what you desire. Be patient. Be consistent. Look at it this way! If something bad is happening, you must deal with it whether you approach it negatively or positively. Can we agree that a negative approach could add more strife to the circumstance? If your answer is yes, moving forward approach every situation and circumstance in your future with nothing but positivity. Have you heard this before: "Be the change you want to see in the world." Hopefully, it has meaning to you now. It's not easy, but it is something to work towards.

Let's recap a little bit!

In chapter 4, I said, "Most children want to be accepted. I must give you my interpretation of "How we get introduced to ourselves or the lack thereof."

If your parents weren't programming you to get to know yourself, they have programmed the total opposite. You have no way to defend yourself against that. You are wired. How many other programs exist from ex-girlfriends/boyfriends or friends overall?

And in Chapter 4, I said, "Following standards by default. You have the right as an individual to do things differently. When I started the process of getting to know myself, I couldn't do that without redefining myself." I learned at some point I needed to reprogram my mind and decide who I was or who I wasn't becoming. Are you continuing to follow default programs or are you taking control? Those mental programs could be ruining your life. Do you wonder what it looks like to allow mental programs you didn't consciously adopt to ruin your life?

Remember this statement: "Living Life by Default"

"This is the adoption of preselected options, styles, trends, fashion, lifestyle, standards, a belief system, or way of life, ideas, or concepts. We are usually conditioned to live like this meaning by being exposed to or spending time out of our lives around something or anyone thing or a specific understanding could influence our decisions. With this said, we are simply not in control of our life if we are living according to these beliefs. We are controlled and/or restricted in our minds and it is normal that most people do not think past commonality. As a matter of fact, you are considered crazy when you do things out of the ordinary."

You know you have the ability of making better decisions with your time, money, and resources, but you continue to do the total opposite. This is a great example. You could change this mental programming by learning new information while surrounding yourself with good examples of people who conduct themselves in a manner you'd like to adopt. You would create a shift in your behavior, habits, and your attitude.

In the Introduction, I said:

"A conscious decision to change is the beginning, but it isn't enough because we, as humans, forget. The wind can blow, and you'll go into a new direction unless a decision to make a change in your life is deeply rooted."

Do you see how the conscious and subconscious mind plays into this? The conscious decision doesn't change the mental programming on the subconscious level unless it has been suggested to the subconscious on a daily basis for about three weeks. So, you cannot simply decide today to make a suggestion to change a mental program and expect the long-term changes as if you have uprooted the seeds from the soil. Imagine trying to intentionally unlearn how to walk or

The Life That Brightens the Light

ride a bike (*assuming you know how to ride a bike*). How difficult would that be? What about something you wanted to quit? How easy or difficult is it to stop a habit you had/have? This isn't applicable to everything, but most habits.

Again, this is why it is commonly known to do a thing consistently for about three weeks. Your subconscious mind has to accept the idea to rewrite the program you have on that topic, but you must be consistent for the new action to be accepted by the subconscious mind. It is easy, but not simple. Why does the subconscious mind give us a hard time rewriting programs? The subconscious mind automating our habits and the individual task we need actuating are the reasons why we can live a stable life. What do I mean?

Imagine being responsible for regulating your body temperature, making sure every individual breath you take is smooth, making your heart beat on time at the right time. What about when you walk or run? Have you ever been drunk before? If you have, that is the perfect example of walking consciously. When your mind is impaired, you can't walk subconsciously. You are forced to do this consciously. You do a lot of walking, right? That would slow you down significantly if you had to consciously walk all the time, right? Look how good of a job your subconscious mind is doing. I am going to assume you can walk on a daily without much thought. How about when your mind is impaired *by way of alcohol and/or substances*? That is why our subconscious mind hates changing or uprooting habits and programs. It gives our lives the stability we need to operate on a daily basis. If our subconscious mind didn't take on these role by way of habitual acts or mental programs, the responsibility would be left to the conscious mind and it would overload and shutdown. The conscious mind cannot handle too much responsibility or it will literally crash and shutdown. So the subconscious mind is usually the one that kicks into action when the conscious mind isn't operating or operational.

You can uproot a mental program you don't want just like you can pick up bad mental programming. You heard the saying, "*Birds of a feather flock together.*" Avoid people you don't want to be like and spend time with those you want to be more like.

This is the end of the conscious and subconscious mind portion of the book. Find good resources to learn more about this topic. You'll literally be learning more about yourself. There are a lot of benefits from gaining this new understanding. Trust me!

Hopefully, this is making you think.

Let's move on to the next chapter.

Chapter 10

Mindset Control

"Hypnosis"

I don't know how you feel about this topic, but I must introduce you to the foundation of hypnosis if you have never been exposed. Again, my mission is to give basic information on the subject. My wish is that you would find a dependable resource and conduct more research on the topic. Let's dig in!

What is hypnosis?

Hypnosis is when your conscious mind moves aside and the critical faculty is bypassed allowing your subconscious mind to be open to positive suggestions for change.

What is the critical faculty? The critical faculty is like a filter and information must pass through your critical faculty before information may enter your belief system, subconscious mind and/or permanent memory. Can you see where this is going? We recently left the topic of the conscious and subconscious mind so it was only right to touch this topic.

So, the conscious mind has four jobs: 1) willpower, 2) temporary memory, 3) analytical, 4) rational thinking. I'll give you an idea of each specific job.

What is willpower? It is the conscious force you apply. An example would be if a salesman were trying to sell you something you shouldn't buy. You want it, but you know it's not something you'll need. You begin to use your willpower to end the conversation with the salesman to remove the opportunity to make a possible transaction despite the temptation. The salesman has gone as far as discounting the item only for today to close the sale. The force that you applied to get rid of the sales guy is called, "Willpower." It took a strong conscious decision to be forceful and firm. That's willpower.

Preconscious Mind –

A great way to describe the preconscious mind is by comparing it to the critical faculty; which both work as a filter. The preconscious mind works as a filter to filter what memories are made conscious versus the critical faculty filters thoughts, ideas and concepts from entering the subconscious mind.

What is temporary memory? Temporary memories are also classified as short-term memories that are in your immediate awareness. In a memory in your preconscious mind, you would need to recall and make it conscious because it is NOT in your immediate awareness. An example would be, "What did you eat yesterday?" You don't immediately remember, so it isn't in your immediate awareness; therefore, it is recalled as a file and opened by consciousness. Another way it can be stated is: after a little thought you pulled that information from your preconscious and brought it to your awareness where your conscious activates the file/memory. If you are inside a restaurant and your party arrives after you've ordered your food. Temporary memories are when you are asked, "What did you just order?" That's a conscious memory because it DOES NOT need to be recalled from your preconscious mind.

Analytical is simply analyzing thoughts, circumstances, questions, demands, and decisions. Before you go outside, you determined it is best to bring a jacket because last time you were outdoors you were very cold. You would like to avoid this circumstance. The subconscious mind doesn't analysis anything. In this case, the subconscious mind didn't analyze the condition of protecting yourself from the cold because the subconscious mind doesn't think or analyze. This determination came from the conscious mind.

Rational thinking is when you analyze information to make a decision. For example, let's say you want to go to a gym. Instead of using analytical thinking which requires brain power and energy, you go with your gut instead of using rational thinking to determine which gym makes the most sense (*price, distance, amount of equipment, timing, and user capacity*). But instead, you go with your gut instinct or intuition (*No Thought*). These are the four jobs of the conscious mind.

Did you know these two parts of the mind have a language? The language of the conscious mind is logical and the language of the subconscious is imaginative. Whenever there is a conflict between the conscious (Logic & Reason) and the subconscious mind (The Imagination), the subconscious mind wins every time. The subconscious mind is the boss.

Do you remember when I stated in the introduction of this book?

"A conscious decision to change is the beginning, but it isn't enough because we, as humans, forget. The wind can blow, and you'll go into a new direction unless a decision to make a change in your life is deeply rooted."

So, basically, you can consciously make a decision to change a habit in your life in the moment, but if you don't entertain this idea long enough for your subconscious mind to accept this change, the change isn't considered, "Deeply rooted." The conscious decision is a start to this process, but it isn't ultimate deciding factor for a long-term impact meaning you might change your actions for the day. However, as soon as you go to sleep and wake up, you will need to continue to have the willpower to consciously contradict the original mental programming.

Let's change gears a little bit. It is easy to find yourself in the middle of a conflict between the two parts of your mind. I'll give you a great example of this mental conflict between the conscious and subconscious parts of the mind.

Let's say for an example:

So, what is hypnosis, again? Hypnosis is when your conscious mind moves aside, and the critical faculty is bypassed allowing your subconscious mind to be open to positive suggestions for change. Do you notice when people are being hypnotized they are usually sleeping or in a sleep state? This is because the conscious mind is shutoff or shutdown. They are not dead so their body is living as well. The ears work. The heart still beats when you are unconscious (*assuming you are alive*) and even while in a coma.

While the conscious mind isn't available, a hypnotist can make suggestions directly to an individual's subconscious mind if he is *personally receptive* to the hypnotist. The subconscious will accept the suggestion as truth regardless of what is suggested, but only if the subject is open to the hypnotist. Imagine a person crying while watching a sad movie in a dark theater? Well, let's talk about that for a second.

Why would a person cry when they know the movie isn't real, and they know every actor is acting? Can you cry on command? It's pretty difficult. I cannot cry on command. Can you? Well, the conscious mind is shutdown while you are watching a movie. Your subconscious mind cannot determine what is reality and what is false. Your subconscious mind believe what you are watching is real therefore when the emotions are meant to be saddening your subconscious controls your emotions and give your body the desire to cry due to the power and control your subconscious have over your emotions. The reason you are crying is because the imagination is the language of the subconscious mind and a movie is visually consumed. This language the movie is speaking to your subconscious is received. In turn, you begin to physically cry because your subconscious mind said to do so.

When a hypnotist uses hypnotic verbiage in order to guide your imagination, they are using the skill of hypnotic language to control what you are visualizing and imagining. Remember, the language of the subconscious mind is imaginative. Remember, when I would lie down at night before going to sleep I'd imagine myself in the lifestyle of a celebrity. I'd literally imagine my future using the power of the

The Life That Brightens the Light

subconscious in order to tap into the law of attraction. So, when the hypnotist gives suggestions and the subconscious mind accepts it, the subconscious acts out the suggestion without any restrictions. Your subconscious mind will make sure you see, hear, and feel what was suggested.

So, if you were given the suggestion that a pen was a very hot piece of iron, when your skin is touched, the subconscious makes sure your body reacts to the touch of the pen as if you were burned. You will see and feel the reaction of the touch of hot iron. The mind is that powerful.

Let's jump off topic for a little bit.

Mesmerized. The definition of mesmerized is to hold the attention of *someone* to the exclusion of all else so to transfix them. Do you know the history behind this word?

Well, this history involves a German man by the name of "Franz Anton Mesmer." Mesmer was a very popular doctor back in the 1700's. He had an interest in astronomy. He theorized the existence of a nature energy transference occurring between all animated and inanimate objects. This is what he called "animal magnetism." The invisible fluid in the body acted according to the laws of magnetism.

He had a different approach to deal with mental illness and other illnesses. He felt he could save patients by rubbing his hands over their shoulders, chest, and their pelvic regions. He had a strong belief that he was using magnets to heal his subjects.

One of his patients made him famous when Dr. Mesmer brought back the sight of one of his clients. This caused people near and far to stand outside of his house hoping to be healed, and he continued to have some influence until the end of the 19th century. The term "mesmerize" was proposed by the Scottish doctor James Braid in 1843 as hypnosis. Dr. Mesmer was on to something, but it was different from his original discovery. Dr. Braid brought our awareness to hypnosis.

The language of the subconscious mind is the imagination, and again it cannot tell what is real and what is false. Everything is real and true to the imaginative mind. If your subconscious doesn't believe it, the critical faculty doesn't allow information that is not believable into the subconscious mind.

Why do you cry when watching a sad movie? You know it's not real. You cry because you are not conscious. If you are not conscious that means you cannot use logic and think to yourself, "This isn't real" and arrest the emotions that overtake you. You must be communicating on an imaginative level. Your subconscious mind believes everything you are seeing and allows your body to feel the emotion. You don't use logic to address the sad feelings because you are not conscious in order to do so.

In hypnosis, a hypnotist will remove the critical faculty to the side and give positive suggestions to your subconscious mind planting a suggestion. You don't get a choice of if you follow the suggestion or not because the subconscious mind doesn't determine what is a good suggestion or a bad one. Once the suggestion enters it is applied to your being.

Think about it! All the programs from your childhood come directly from your family and the environment you were raised in. What kind of programs do you think exist? Do you think these programs have determined what you do or do not pay your attention too as an adult? I think so. What lifestyle or mental programming did you adopt through the infancy – 7 year-old phase?

The movies, television shows, and commercials you watch on television have influenced you as well. What kind of programming could have been uploaded to your hard-drive? If the subconscious language is imaginative, can a good storyteller influence your decisions like a movie or television show? A salesman uses the skill of storytelling in order to bypass your critical faculty in order to persuade you to make buying decisions. You are considered an impulse buyer. Marketing content including billboards, ads, commercials, sells pitches, and presentations is created with these same techniques. We have so many tactics playing at our mind. How many things are in place to protect our mind? That is your job, and if you haven't been doing it, you have adopted many programs that don't work in your favor.

Question everything and remove unnecessary boundaries. However, this decision to grow will open new doors, new possibilities, new decisions, a new attitude, a new walk, and a new talk. When you feel limited in your life you need to simply expand the walls of your subconscious mind more into the realm of possibility.

Let's talk about the control of our conscious ability versus the ability of our subconscious mind. What if you could consciously think something and instantly have it in a tangible state of reality? Well, we are so powerful as living beings we needed something to contain our weapon, tool, and power (*our minds*). Our subconscious mind walls our conscious mind. Why? How stable would our lives be if we could consciously think something and instantly have it in a tangible form in reality? Our lives wouldn't be as stable, but why?

Example:

Imagine if you could think 1-million dollars and it appeared instantly by way of the law of attraction. Well, there is a flip side to the coin because when you think evil things, they happen instantly (it works with the law of polarity/just because it's negative doesn't eliminate the ability to create). Imagine how conflicted our lives would be. This reality wouldn't be sustainable so we have our walls. What are the walls to our consciousness?

Basically, our conscious cannot make things into reality without a filter to protect us as living-beings so we would create with a strong intention. *It's not as simple as think and it becomes reality.* This is why it takes so long to re-write the subconscious programs in our minds. The intention can be focused long enough for the subconscious mind to accept and re-write our new belief and then create it in a tangible form in reality. Then, 1) it is accepted by our subconscious so it can be manifested or at least begin the process of the law of attraction to do what it does best. It is believed that the subconscious mind is somehow connected to the energy, the earth, and God himself to help bring into reality what we truly desire, even if it is harmful to our goals, priorities, well-being and our futures. The subconscious mind is the boss. It is powerful. Learn how to use it for your benefit.

Let's summarize this topic.

The subconscious mind is the wall that contains consciousness and the subconscious mind acts as a filter to reject our ability to instantly call things into exist with a simple, conscious thought. Let's call it our "Checks and Balances." You can manipulate your reality, but you must change the subconscious mind to attract the things you really want to manifest into reality. We don't want the ability to do this consciously. The subconscious is the door to more or fewer possibilities depending on how you use the gift. How do you change your mind? How do you expand those walls?

How do you make the box that houses your consciousness bigger? A great place to start is being more aware of what goes into your eyes and ears. Control your exposure to manipulating individuals that can successfully use the art of storytelling or the use of the hypnotic language. Control your exposure to marketing content because they have a specific motive, and it's not in your favor in the name of mental programs. Stay away from negative individuals because their actions affect your reality and your subconscious programming in a negative way. Surround yourself with people you want to model yourself after. In addition, you can use the law of polarity. Include more exposure to positive information in your life, your surroundings, and allow your subconscious mind to soak up good principles and information. Get some therapy or counseling to determine if there are any past traumas destroying your life that you don't know exist. You need to know to understand that this is possible. Protect yourself and your future. Self-sabotaging behavior stems from this effect. You don't always have to be aware of it for it to be active in your mental programming. As I mentioned earlier, if you wish to seek counseling the person I would recommend is Latoya Oates. You can find her online at:

www.NewRulezAcademy.com

The Life That Brightens the Light

A very creative way most individuals, including myself, download better programming into our subconscious mind is by using recordings and visualization videos. This video will have a brainwashing component on the topic you select to play on a daily basis. An example of this would be opening YouTube and typing into the search box "Positive Affirmations for Subconscious Mind." You can also search for specific affirmations for your subconscious programming such as "positive affirmations for more money." Or for making the right connections, positive self-talk, I am NOT a failure, I always win, and I am worthy. Listen to one and get an idea of what they sound like. Try a video for three-weeks. Watch how your subconscious will begin to work in your favor. It works.

You can also combat negative coming from your being as well. Pay attention to your thoughts and the things you say out of your mouth. Small corrections can lead to big changes most definitely if you are programmed in a negative manner. You can go as far as viewing money differently. The point is to have a strong intention of creating a better version of yourself. Remember I mentioned that you cannot use your conscious mind to recreate your reality so the subconscious mind is the wall that contains your conscious mind? You must reprogram the files inside your subconscious mind to call into existence healthier programs; you, plant for a different harvest which changes the seeds; you, plant for a different harvest. We are still talking about your mind.

Also, control the music, movies, shows, and videos you watch and listen to on a daily basis. They have an impact and take a toll as well. Go back and listen to the lyrics to the music you listen too. What is it building in your life? Do you recite those lyrics? What are you manifesting? I think you are starting to get the picture.

Chapter 11

Closing Statement

"The End"

I have shared a lot of concepts with you in this book, and I hope a new person is beginning to arise. I promise you will never be the same again. Life should make more sense to you at this point—at least in the aspect of creating success. You are powerful, and you are in control even if you don't know you are because you have contributed to everything you have and don't have up until this point. You read this book. Your life matters! You matter! Make the time you have left count. You can still make a difference even if the difference is for others. You have a story. Remember to make your mess your message. Go out into the world and take on the things you once thought were impossible. Everything was impossible until someone figured it out. You are never stuck.

I am going to close with this idea. Lazy people make people like you and I look good. What do I mean? Well, everyone can do the impossible. An example would be the track star that doesn't have legs or the swimmer who is missing limbs. Look at the greatest basketball players in the world or the greatest singers in the world. All of these people that achieved the highest level of success for their industries have everything we have, but it's up to us to apply ourselves and strive for the top.

Let's say, "You want to be the fastest swimmer in the world." If you give all of your time, effort, and energy to this one idea and never quit, 10 years from today you can be recognized as one of the fastest swimmers in the world. However, this isn't your goal. You can find the drive necessary to be the best at anything you choose. Lazy people or average people don't care to apply themselves in such a way to do the impossible. This is a choice to stay average, but everyone has what they need to be more than average. So when someone chooses to give his life, time, effort, and energy to be the best at something, it makes him appear unique, great, and even superhuman. He gets the recognition that comes with being labeled as the best or the unbeatable. We all have the potential to be great at something, but society prefers to be average. If you choose not to be average you can be the best. You can be looked upon as the greatest. The Michael Jordan's and the Kobe's of the world are out there giving it everything they have in order to one day become the next Kobe. The Steve Jobs of the world are out there right now failing and experiencing life trying to figure it out in order to become the next Steve Jobs of the world. Finding examples are easy because someone is great in every sport, industry, job, skill, and title.

The people that choose to be average make these people look good because average people choose not to apply themselves and look at the greats. Becoming super rich and wealthy is impossible, or the greats of the world look at being the best in the world as if it isn't impossible for everyone. With the right mindset, drive, and enough time, you can literally be anything. I am hoping my book is the spark of the next Steve Jobs, Michael Jordan, Kobe Bryant, Michael Jackson, or whoever you are to become. The point is this--it's possible. There are a ton of good examples out there in the world for everything under the sun. Choose your lane and be great. The people that refuse to work themselves to the bone are out there right now giving up and taking breaks and making you look good. So I'll say it again, "Lazy people make people like you and me look good." Don't be a quitter. Don't be average. Don't take breaks. Be great because you have everything you need in order to do so. If you need permission, I just gave it to you. I learned this concept while out to lunch with a group of dancers, tap-dancers, and musicians. We were all in separate industries looking up to the best in our industries. Everyone we discussed had applied many of the concepts in this book. They didn't make excuses. They didn't quit. They never stopped learning. They eventually made it to the top, and some slowed down after becoming the best while some continued to challenge themselves. But what they had in common was that they were considered the best or top for their industry. The "Bachata Crew" is responsible for helping me discover this idea. Average people have what it takes to be everything they desire, but for whatever reason, they won't apply themselves. This is not going to be you. Is there something wrong with being average? No, because only we can determine what success is to us. However, if the faster time recorded for the one mile run in the world is 4-minutes, it wouldn't hurt if you decided to drop it to 2:30. There are rewards that come from doing the impossible and being one of the best to ever do it. People even get rewarded for just being good at any one thing, so you don't always have to be the richest. Just be good, and when you get there, don't get comfortable. Ask yourself--What's next?

That was the last and finally concept of this book. Thank you so much for reading, "The life that brightens the light." I hope you understand the title now. I want my life to brighten the light that is already inside you. I just want you to shine brighter. Hopefully, this book will do just that. Be great. Be you!

The End!